Staging a Miracle

A Practical Parent's Guide

To Surviving an Autism Diagnosis

Jason D. Eden, M.B.A.

DEDICATION

This book is dedicated to my wife, my daughter, my son, and to the amazing team of therapists and teachers who each had a part in making our journey the success it is today. I love you all more than you can ever know.

Jason D. Eden, M.B.A.

CONTENTS

Chapter 1: How to Avoid Wasting Time and Money 4

    The 5 Biggest Time Traps in the Autism World..5

    How to Avoid Time Traps 10

Chapter 2: How to Evaluate Autism Treatments 12

    4 Most Destructive False Beliefs Regarding Autism...............................12

    The 4 Types of Therapies Every Family Should Consider........................22

    How to Know Which Therapies are Right for Your Child 26

    The #1 Reason Kids with Autism Don't Make Progress 28

Chapter 3: How to Navigate Legal and Political Issues 31

    The Top 3 Mistakes People Make When Dealing With School Systems
    and Government Agencies..31

    3 Indicators of a Good School District.....................................37

    8 Things Every Parent *Must* Do To Prepare 38

How to Deal with the Rest of the World..42

    Understand Your Rights in Neighborhood and Housing Disputes 42

    3 Common Mistakes to Avoid In Housing Situations 43

    How to Take Time Off of Work for Therapy or Training 44

    2 Commonly Overlooked Options for Funding Therapy Expenses 45

How To Avoid Getting Scammed 47

How To Deal With Family and Friends 48

Chapter 4: Two Weeks That Can Change Your Life 50

What the Program Does for Parents 52

8 Critical Things the TouchPoint Parent Training Program Teaches .. 53

3 Critical Steps To Ensure the Best Possible Result 54

5 Hidden Ways to Love Your Child With Autism 58

Chapter 5: How to Build an Effective Therapy Program 61

How to Choose a Therapist 61

What to Do if You Choose the Wrong Therapist 62

9 Personalities You Should Seek Out for Your Team 63

2 Critical Steps to Engage Older Siblings 71

3 Ways to Stretch Therapy Supply Dollars 73

Goals in Concrete, Plans in Sand 76

ACKNOWLEDGMENTS

I am but an aggregator of a great deal of knowledge passed on to me by innumerable therapists, research organizations, and life strategists who taught me how to think about my son's situation through consultation, seminars, books, and web sites. Special thanks to my lovely bride, Melynda, for your unending support even when you weren't sure I knew what I was doing. (You were right, I often didn't.) Additional thanks to some key folks who played a big role in our lives during those early years, in no particular order: Sarah, Tim, Nathan, Kyler, Julia, Carrie, Birka, Holly, Mary, Bob, Phil, Marc, Janice, Edie, and Kay, as well as innumerable other friends, therapists, and family members who gave us encouragement and hope. Awesome groups whose work I heavily leveraged include TouchPoint Autism Services, the Thompson Center for Autism and Neurodevelopmental Disorders, and the Washington University's, Olin Business School Executive MBA Program leadership and strategy departments. Finally, a huge thank you to Mrs. Teresa Dixon. Your influence in my early life was and is felt powerfully in my son's recovery. You helped me see that each person has the capacity to choose their own paths in life, and this is a lesson I am passing on to my own children. You'll recognize your influence deeply embedded in these pages.

PROLOGUE

This book is an easy-to-follow road map for navigating the twists and turns your life will take after receiving an Autism-related diagnosis. If this book had existed when we first received our son's diagnosis, I could have avoided countless hours of worry and frustration, numerous strategic mistakes, and thousands of dollars in unnecessary expenses. I have no doubt that Timothy's continuing emergence from Autism could have been a smoother experience had I known at the beginning what I know now. This book exists to help you avoid the mistakes while taking advantage of the lessons learned.

For a parent who has just learned that their child is affected with one of the many ASDs, the amount of potential misinformation available is staggering and can be harmful to your child's health and your emotional and financial resources. I distinctly remember those first few days and weeks of searching for information, for a roadmap that we could use to navigate this new and treacherous journey in our lives. What I found instead was a jungle of conflicting claims and information.

Families afflicted with Autism are preyed upon by groups of "medical professionals," social movements, and agencies with official-sounding names that make claims that have been scientifically debunked for years, charge thousands of dollars for highly-questionable tests and treatments, and then blame parents for not doing it right when their solutions inevitably fail, or on the other hand, try to make you feel guilty for doing what is necessary to help your child improve. It's a dangerous and unfriendly world for an emotionally-stricken parent looking for answers.

Let me give you some hope. Regardless of where your child is right now, their level of functioning, or the severity with which an ASD has affected them, odds are strong that they *can* improve. There *are* well-trodden paths to success that hundreds of thousands have gone down before you. There *are* emerging therapies based on solid scientific research that are helping children with an ASD recover to levels that would have been unheard of just a decade ago. While nothing can take away the anguish of receiving an ASD diagnosis, take heart: there has never been a better time in history for your child to have the best chance possible at a life that helps them meet their fullest potential. This will not be an easy journey, but that was guaranteed from the moment you first suspected there might be something different about your child. Let's walk through this together, and let me help you set the stage for your own personal miracle.

Chapter 1: How to Avoid Wasting Time and Money

"You cannot change what you do not acknowledge. And what you do not acknowledge is going to get worse until you do."
|– *Dr. Phil McGraw, <u>Life Strategies</u>, 1999*

One of the hardest things for many parents of a child with an Autism Spectrum Disorder (ASD) is to accept what has happened, and during this process precious time is lost – particularly in the early developmental years – when significant progress could be made. Behavioral psychologists call this phenomenon "perceptual defense" – the inability to perceive things that are too much to bear or that threaten your sense of identity. For victims of terrible tragedies, this can be a blessing. For families with a special-needs child, it can be terribly damaging.

The sooner you accept the fact that your child has or might have an ASD, and the earlier you intervene, the better your chances of success will be! Can you imagine learning that your child had leukemia or a congenital heart defect and choosing to ignore it? Unfortunately, because most ASDs aren't detected through biological testing today, many families – or certain members of those families – do just that when an ASD becomes evident. Failing to admit what is happening has the potential to destroy or severely injure everyone you love. I have seen it happen, and have heard countless similar stories. It is tragic.

Unfortunately, the problem is often made worse because the people around us are too nice. Well-meaning doctors and other early childhood professionals, not wanting to cause unnecessary concern or panic, will utter phrases like "All children develop differently, it's nothing to be concerned about" or "It's just a phase – he'll probably grow out of it." Friends will regale you with stories about little Jimmy who didn't talk until he was five years old and is now a neurosurgeon, or little Susie who fixated on dolls as a child and is now a world-renowned fashion designer. They all intend to make you feel better. Unfortunately, their words and actions can cause you to question your judgment and thus delay getting treatment.

The 5 Biggest Time Traps in the Autism World

The "This Can't Be Happening" Trap

If you are early in your journey or have never really accepted the truth about your child, this is the most important thing you will read in this book. You cannot defeat an enemy you do not acknowledge exists. An ASD has claimed your child, or a part of him/her, and if you want to have a shot at getting them back in your life, you have to take this first critical step.

If this is you, please, for your child's sake, repeat after me: "I have a child with an Autism spectrum disorder." Admitting is hard, but now it's time to move forward and do something about it. Unfortunately, even after coming to grips with this harsh reality, there are still many common time, money, and energy traps that keep us from moving forward in the best possible way.

The "What Exactly" Trap

ASDs cover a wide range of symptoms, behaviors, and social/emotional challenges. Far too many people get hung up on what the exact diagnosis for their child is going to be, and spend a lot of time and money in an effort to hear what they want to hear. For example, I know of families who feel much better about their child's situation when their doctors give them a diagnosis of PDD-NOS (Pervasive Developmental Disorder – Not Otherwise Specified) rather than Autism Spectrum Disorder, and will spend weeks and months, if necessary, getting the "right" diagnosis. "My child doesn't have Autism, it's just PDD-NOS," they'll say, and for some reason feel better about the situation.

If the words on the piece of paper the doctor handed out would make a difference, then I too would spend the time to fight for my son's diagnosis to be changed to PDD-NOS. Unfortunately, that diagnosis would not change my child's behaviors, nor would it affect the types of treatment my child needs. What it *would* do is muddy the waters for the school systems and government agencies that provide assistance for Timothy's recovery. PDD-NOS in some cases is an accurate diagnosis of an Autism-like disorder that lacks some of the qualities of true Autism, but in other cases is a cop-out – an unwillingness to admit the truth.

At the end of the day, the official diagnosis doesn't matter. "What" your child is afflicted with may be called any number of things, but what it is called should not affect how you approach treatment. Thus, watch yourself carefully to make sure you don't obsess over "what exactly" your child has once you've started down the ASD path. It doesn't do any good, and may well distract you from more important matters.

The "Why" Trap

Perhaps far more damaging than the "What Exactly" trap is the "Why" trap. This is the phase that every family goes through trying to figure out why their child is afflicted with an ASD, and unfortunately, many people get stuck here. There are lots of theories as to the causes of ASDs, but the overwhelming scientific evidence and the latest research indicates that at least 80% of cases are "Essential" Autism, which have a distinct genetic cause. The other 20% of cases are "Complex" Autism. These cases are almost always accompanied by significant physical abnormalities and significantly lower IQ scores, and may have an environmental cause. If your child does not have significant challenges other than Autism, odds are they fall into the "Essential" category.

Regardless of whether you accept the science or not, the bigger question is this: Who cares? If years from now scientists discover that Vitamin D deficiency is a contributing factor, or that too much ketchup consumed during pregnancy was the primary cause for ASDs, what good is that going to be to your child? You can't go back and fix the cause. It's OK to ask and wonder why, but too many families get so hung up on figuring this out or finding someone to blame that they don't have the energy or resources they need to address the needs of their child in the present. Stop obsessing over why this happened, and focus on what's important: How to move forward and give your child the best chance in life they can possibly get. Move on! It's the best thing you can do for your child.

The "I Can't" Trap

Another common problem I have observed are families that refuse to believe they can make a difference, and thus instead of dealing head-on with the situation they will simply accept the current reality as inevitable. For example, I once had a conversation with a well-meaning mother who described the impossibility of dealing with her seven-year-old son. When I asked for an example, she told me that he would watch three seconds of a certain video, rewind it, and watch those same three seconds over and over again. This behavior was keeping her from making any progress with him. The conversation went something like this:

- I proposed that she move the VCR out of his reach.
- She responded that he would climb to get to it.
- I proposed that she lock it in a cabinet.
- She responded that he would find the key to get to it.
- I proposed that she lock the room that it was kept in, etc.
- She responded that no matter what she did, he would find a way to beat her.

That kind of thinking leads to enablement, not recovery. **As long as your child is a child, there is almost *no* battle you should not be able to win**. You are bigger, stronger, faster, and smarter than they are – for a while anyway – and you should press those advantages as hard as possible during their early recovery years.

The "I Can't" trap also manifests itself in other ways:

- "I can't afford therapy..."
- "I can't fight the system..."
- "I can't relocate to a better area..."

And many, many more.

The bottom line is this: You *can* do all of these things – and more – and you would if you understood the power it might have to improve your child's life and believed the outcomes possible. You would find the time and money for either therapy or to equip yourself with the skills necessary to help your child recover yourself. You would fight schools, neighborhoods, and government agencies that tried to deny you services. You would do what you had to do to move to an area where better services were available. You would lock the VCR in a safe and only take it out when you could control it until the target behavior had subsided. But you first have to believe that the sacrifices you make will be worth it in the end.

Let's get real here: You may have to move to a different neighborhood, or even a different state. You may have to learn to survive on a single income, or take a lower-paying job with more flexible hours, and thus significantly downgrade your lifestyle. You may have to spend yourself to the verge of bankruptcy – maybe beyond. **This is a war, and one you cannot afford to lose!** An ASD has claimed your child, and if you have a chance – any chance – at any type of recovery, you have to be willing to restructure your entire life around defeating this enemy!

This book will point you towards many of the tools that will be instrumental in your journey, but you have to be willing to make significant sacrifices that to an outside observer might seem extreme. If you can avoid "I Can't" thinking and start critically and creatively thinking of ways around those "impossible" issues, you'll move a lot farther a lot faster down your child's road to recovery, and give them the best life possible. You *can* make a difference, you *can* win the battles you choose to fight. You *will* have to make sacrifices. Help is out there, and hope runs high! You have to be willing to accept your situation and move forward, believing that your child can get better and that you *can* make a significant difference in his or her life. The sooner you come to grips with this, the sooner you will be able to start making the tough decisions necessary to beat this thing. Believe you can!

The "Do It All" Trap

The flip-side of the "I Can't" trap is the "Do It All" trap. In this situation, a family chooses to attack Autism from every angle at once in the hopes that something sticks and makes progress. Families in this state will try anything, pay for any test or treatment, no matter how outlandish the claims might be, on the off-chance that the next thing will be the silver bullet that they've been looking for to magically cure their child.

The downside to this approach is just like all of the other traps: wasted time, money, and energy. Not all therapies are appropriate for all kids with an ASD. At best, the time and money spent on unneeded or inappropriate therapies could have been spent on a more effective treatment. At worst, some therapies can actually cause physical harm and create new medical problems that otherwise would not have existed.

You should be willing to do whatever it takes to get your child closer to recovery, but that doesn't mean you have to do everything that's out there – not by a long shot. In this book, we will present a way to think about therapies that will allow you to select the most appropriate ones for your child. Do everything necessary, but make sure what you're doing is really necessary.

How to Avoid Time Traps

All of these traps all have a common thread: the inability to correctly prioritize how you spend your time, money, and emotional energy. Thus, one step towards the cure for these traps is to create a list of all of the things in your life at a high level, order these things according to their importance, and consciously make decisions accordingly. For example, here is the list I came up with early on in Timothy's journey to recovery in an attempt to avoid the "I Can't" trap:

My Priorities:

- My relationship with God
- My relationship with my spouse
- My relationship with my kids
- Timothy's recovery
- My relationship with other family members
- My relationships with my friends
- What I do for a living
- Where I worship
- My financial security
- My personal fitness
- Where I live
- Where I go to school
- My retirement plans
- Etc.

The upshot of actually making this list was that it helped me make decisions based on trade-offs I was forced to make. Essentially, if a decision would positively affect Timothy's recovery without affecting my overall relationship with God, my spouse, and Timothy and his sister, it did not matter how it affected anything else in my life – I went for it. The "I Can't" trap was effectively neutralized. You may prioritize differently than

I do. I'm not insisting that my list is the right list for everyone, but you should have a list like this to help guide you when you face a tough decision.

If you do, it makes it easier to build a locked shelf for the VCR, or in our particular case, live as a one-car family, replace your interior furniture with plastic shelving and drawers intended for basements and garages, become landlords because you have to move to a better school district before your house can sell, or add locks at six-feet up to every interior door in the house, and for those doors that's not practical, remove them, as well as every door on every toy your child has. Your child's recovery is more important than how easy it is for you to watch a movie in the afternoon, how convenient it is to go places, how aesthetically pleasing your home's interior might be, and the pain of answering the "where are all the doors?" questions people will ask.

You can avoid the "Why" trap by simply accepting what has happened, performing some medical and genetic tests in order to rule out or confirm certain biomedical or environmental causes, and then simply move on. Once you've ruled out biomedical indications (and thus treatments), accept that it's likely just plain old genetics and, again, just move on.

The "Do It All" trap is a little trickier, since we tend to equate doing "more" with doing "better." **Here you have to realize that every decision you make, every moment spent in one type of therapy, is a moment that you cannot spend in another.** If you had $1,000 to invest and had two guaranteed, risk-free options to invest in – one with a 2% rate of return and another with a 15% rate of return, you wouldn't want to invest in the first one just because it existed – you'd put all of your money in the investment with the 15% guarantee. Even if you have virtually unlimited funds (which we did *not*), you cannot reclaim lost time. Make sure that you are doing your best to critically analyze the therapy options (investments) available and spend every precious minute and dollar you have on the ones that are likely to have the biggest long-term impact. There are a number of options, but fortunately you shouldn't have to guess which ones you should pursue. This book will help you figure these issues out.

Chapter 2: How to Evaluate Autism Treatments

One of the first things a person typically does when they learn of a loved one with a serious malady is to learn everything they can about it. In the case of ASDs, there is an over-abundance of information available in books, on Web sites, and from innumerable professionals from widely ranging fields of study. An unfortunate truth about much of this information is that it's simply garbage! Another unfortunate truth is that it can be difficult to tell the difference between the true scientific data and the impassioned but misguided multitudes or the outright snake-oil salesmen. What makes it even more difficult is that many who fall under all three categories are parts of the same well-known groups, and many of them are doctors.

4 Most Destructive False Beliefs Regarding Autism

The harsh truth is even popular and highly regarded autism advocacy and research groups like Defeat Autism Now! (hereafter DAN!) and the related Autism Research Institute have trouble sorting out the time, money, and energy-wasting cranks from the rational, scientifically-based individuals whose information and work truly add value. Just because a person is a medical doctor, even one that specializes in Autism "treatments," doesn't mean they're not a snake-oil salesperson out to fleece you for every nickel you have. Just because an impassioned celebrity claims that every child with an ASD should eat a certain restricted diet or forego vaccinations doesn't make it so.

The purpose of this chapter is to help you take a look at some of the more controversial topics in the Autism world and think critically about them. The main thing to remember is that your analysis should be based on evidence – real, scientific evidence – not fear, emotion, desperation, anecdotes, or parental testimonies based on placebo effects. Your child's recovery rides on you knowing what *not* to do just as much as what to do.

False Belief #1: Vaccinations Cause Autism

The statistics are eye-opening: today, somewhere around 1 in 100 children born in the U.S. will be diagnosed with an ASD. The number of diagnoses has risen dramatically in the last few decades. Consequently, it has been during this time period that the number of vaccines that are given to infants and young children has dramatically increased. It doesn't help that in some children Autism doesn't manifest itself until around 18 months of age, a time period in which some of these vaccines are typically administered. To many, this correlation is a smoking gun that points to vaccines as a primary cause for Autism. Some of these folks are high-profile celebrities who have children on the spectrum, whose impassioned pleas and real-life struggles make it easy to believe that their claims and beliefs are true, and that we could eliminate Autism if we were only to stop vaccinating our children.

Really? I mean, really?

This is an excellent example of the need to think critically about an issue and to look at what research actually tells us, rather than rely on circumstantial evidence or emotional pleas. The results of following this line of reasoning could be a catastrophic increase in preventable illnesses from whooping cough to the measles. Remember, life before the inauguration of vaccinations wasn't some sort of a mythic 'Golden Age' to which we ought to be seeking to return – death rates from what are now easily preventable childhood illnesses were incredibly high. (There's a *reason* vaccinations were considered to be a giant leap forward.) This is a high-stakes situation, so it's important to carefully consider the facts:

For many years, anti-vaccine activists pointed to themirosal, a preservative that contained a substantial portion of mercury. Mercury poisoning is said to have many of the same symptoms as Autism. Thus, themirosal was cast as the villain by many in the anti-vaccine camp. Thinking critically about this theory, one would naturally come to the conclusion that if we could just get rid of themirosal, Autism rates would decrease – right?

The credibility of this theory was put to the test. In California, themirosal was removed from nearly all childhood vaccines by 2001. If the theory was true, the years following should have resulted in a dramatic decrease in ASD rates in young children. However, the rates of ASD diagnoses steadily *increased*. Denmark had done the same thing nearly a decade earlier, yet found that their Autism rates increased as well.

These constitute simple tests, but were powerfully effective: themirosal fails as a culprit. Unfortunately, many who made a great business out of anti-themirosal treatments or those who desperately clung to that as their "Why" trap continue to claim that themirosal is the primary cause, despite the overwhelming evidence to the contrary. Unfortunately, this pattern is repeated often in the world of Autism activism, and helps suck thousands of families deeply into "Why" and "Do It All" traps.

Another target of the anti-vaccine crowd is the MMR vaccine, which is a single-shot vaccination for the Measles, Mumps, and Rubella (German measles). This vaccine has the unfortunate distinction of being administered around 12-18 months of age, which is again about the time that many children begin exhibiting a regression into ASD. The theory goes that the MMR vaccine contains live viruses that individually might not be problematic, but administered at the same time can cause an inflammation of the gut that allows toxic substances to enter the bloodstream, resulting in Autism.

Once again, this supposed link between MMR and Autism has been intensely researched in the scientific community, and any wide-spread link has been soundly debunked by an overwhelming amount of evidence and scrutiny. MMR was introduced in the U.S. in 1971, yet it wasn't until the 1990s that the "alarming" increase in Autism was detected – the facts just don't line up. It's still not enough for those who make a living by scaring folks away from vaccines, or those caught in the MMR "Why" trap, but by any objective, evidence-based standard, MMR fails as a culprit.

When those two arguments have failed, the anti-vaccine crowd falls back to a vague, "too many vaccines in the world" stance. They say that vaccines are unnecessary and potentially dangerous, and so should be avoided, even in the lack of evidence of a causal link between vaccines and ASDs.

What?

Again, let's take a look at the facts. Throughout history, fear surrounding vaccines has led to increased incidence of the diseases they were intended to treat. Many people today don't realize the dangers implicit in long-forgotten illnesses like the measles. The fact is the measles can cause complications such as pneumonia and encephalitis (an infection that can cause permanent brain injury). In the last major measles outbreak in the U.S., 20 percent of children infected with measles were hospitalized, and 1 in 400 died.

In addition to measles, children who are not vaccinated are at severely increased risk for illnesses such as diphtheria, tetanus, pertussis (whooping cough), mumps, polio, meningitis, chickenpox, and hepatitis, just to name a few. Complications of these illnesses include paralysis, brain damage, hearing loss, blindness, pneumonia, sterilization, convulsions, and death.

So on one hand you have conclusive evidence that vaccines are not a significant risk for ASDs. On the other hand you have conclusive, historical evidence that vaccinations save lives and prevent lots of other dangerous medical conditions. This one is a no-brainer: **get your kids vaccinated!** It doesn't matter what a celebrity or a group of medical professionals might say or believe - if it's not backed up by evidence, don't buy into their claims. Especially when dealing with vaccinations; there's simply too much at stake.

False Belief #2: Genetics Has Little to Do With Autism

Overwhelmingly, science has indicated that the primary cause of ASDs is genetic and hereditary in nature for the vast majority of diagnoses in which major physical abnormalities are not present. Research indicates that about 80% of autism cases are caused by genetics, while the other 20% may be caused by some unidentified environmental factor. Unfortunately, none of the commonly-cited environmental causes seem to be the culprit for those 20%. Unless your child has obvious physical abnormalities and intelligence deficits outside of the Autism diagnosis though, you are facing a genetically induced foe.

There are a number of potential causes or combinations of factors that may be causes. These factors include genetic variations in DNA, genes that affect the formation and function of synapses in the brain, microdeletions in chromosomes, and the age of the mother and father when the child is conceived. Children born into families with a history of schizophrenia, depression, or personality disorders also receive ASD diagnoses more frequently than the general population.

Perhaps most telling, however, are studies done on Autism rates in twins. In pairs of identical twins, who share an identical genetic code, when one twin is diagnosed with Autism the chances that the other twin will also receive an ASD diagnosis is somewhere between 60% and 96%. In non-identical twins, who do *not* share an identical genetic code, the same study showed the second sibling had a 0% to 24% chance of receiving an ASD diagnosis. Thus, there is an incredibly strong link between genetics and ASDs.

False Belief #3: Autism is Caused by My Child's Diet or Allergies

We're getting ready to tackle a sacred cow of the Autism world: Biomedical interventions, and specifically here the Gluten-Free / Casein Free Diet (hereafter the GFCF Diet or just "the Diet"). While there are actually several special diets that biomedical proponents advocate, the GFCF Diet is by far the most common. I will use this discussion to develop a framework for evaluating the myriad biomedical treatments for ASDs that exist today. There are far too many of them to address each one specifically in this book, but the general approach to any treatment option, and especially expensive and risky biomedical treatments, should be the same.

Groups such as the Autism Research Institute advocate the Diet as an important part of the treatment for every child with Autism. It is an incredibly restrictive diet and lifestyle to follow, specialized food to support the Diet is extremely expensive, and the Diet has a number of potential health risks such as decreased bone thickness and malnutrition if not monitored closely. The stakes are high from both a time and money standpoint, as well as a health standpoint. We need to pay attention to the science.

What is the GFCF Diet? Simply put, it is the complete elimination of gluten, found in wheat, barley, rye, etc.; and casein, which is found in milk. More recently, corn products and soy products have been added to the list of no-no's. Advocates of the Diet proclaim that even trace amounts of these products, which includes wheat products used to dust raisins and french fries, can result in negative outcomes. Embarking on this journey is a monumental task. A parent must constantly be on guard for almost any normal food, and sudden mood swings or undesired behaviors can often be blamed on something being ingested that was on the no-list – or so say advocates of the Diet.

Why go to all of this trouble? There are two major reasons given by GFCF advocates:

1) These foods are common food allergens
2) Chemical reactions induced by these foods can cause severe behaviors that are typically associated with ASDs

Advocates of the Diet point to thousands of testimonials, including several popular books on Autism, with stories of families that have used the Diet to successfully treat, and sometimes even cure their child with an ASD! This is a no-brainer, right?

Once again, the problem lies in the science, or lack thereof in support of the GFCF Diet. Most of the research that has been done to support the GFCF Diet has been "single-blind" research in which either the researcher or the parents of the children involved in the study were aware of the study, its intended outcomes, and whether or not they were a part of the research group being tested or the control group that was being used as a comparison. In these studies, someone expects a certain outcome from a certain individual, and lo and behold, that outcome (in this case, a reduction in typical behaviors associated with Autism) is often observed. This is called "bias" on the part of the researcher, and a "placebo effect" on the part of the family in the study, many of whom are likely caught in the "Why" trap and are thus looking for a cause other than genetics that they can hang their hat on. Both of these problems seriously cloud the validity of any single-blind research study.

In a double-blind study, neither the researcher nor anyone associated with the subjects knows who is a part of the research group and who is a part of the control group until after the study is completed. Interestingly, **in these types of studies, the Diet has not been shown to have any affect whatsoever on typical behaviors associated with Autism.** One should be skeptical, at best, regardless of their claims of thousands of cures. Keep in mind, TV evangelists "cure" people of a variety of incurable diseases on a weekly basis, yet for some reason these people never seem to make it onto major cable TV talk shows. It should give one pause.

Let me be very clear here: I am *not* saying you should not consider the Diet, but I *am* saying that you should have a good reason in place before embarking on the journey, and there are methods to determine if this is right for you and your child. One way to test and see if you should consider the GFCF diet is to have a few simple, relatively inexpensive allergy tests done to determine whether or not your child is allergic to these types of foods. If they are, then regardless of whether they treat autistic behaviors or not, you certainly wouldn't want to exacerbate an allergic condition. That said, if no allergies exist, why would you take on such a drastic lifestyle change with its associated health risks?

One of the arguments made to counter negative allergy tests are "food sensitivities" as opposed to allergies. In other words, if the tests don't indicate a need for the Diet, you should still do it anyway, just in case. At this point, the Diet stops looking like a therapy and starts looking like the practice of a cult. Think about it this way: if you or your spouse had a biopsy on tissue that you thought might be cancerous and the test came back negative, would you go ahead and do chemotherapy and radiation – "just in case?" Of course not! In the Autism community, however, this is an all-too-common manifestation of the "Do It All" trap I mentioned earlier in the book. Remember, the Diet is actually *harmful* if it is unnecessary. The food is very expensive, and there are health risks. In addition, every moment and dollar you spend pursuing one course of action is a moment and dollar you cannot spend on another. If there's no evidence to support implementing the Diet for your child, you should not feel obligated to go down such a difficult path out of fear.

Another way the GFCF Diet is used is to treat a condition known as "leaky gut" – which in reality is an extreme and potentially fatal stage in the development of Celiac disease. If your child has Celiac disease, you should absolutely consider the Diet as part of your therapy regimen. Again, however, your child can be tested for Celiac disease. If you're concerned, get it done, and know for sure. If it's not there, and no gluten or casein allergies exist, then there is no scientific evidence that you should subject your child to a GFCF Diet. Again, given the associated health risks, in addition to the time, money, and energy you would waste making sure

19

everything your child consumed was allowed, you should by all means avoid going down this road under those conditions.

One thing that I find disingenuous about many in the GFCF Diet crowd (as well as many other biomedical approaches) is that they advocate using the Diet in conjunction with other treatments such as behavioral therapy and relationship development therapies. The problem with that approach is this: if you start two treatments at the same time and your child improves, how do you know which one of them is working, if both of them are working, or if either one would be less effective without the other? There's no way to know.

By advocating the Diet in conjunction with other therapies from the start, proponents set up a situation where they can potentially take credit for the good being done by the other therapy, whereas if progress is not found, blame can be placed on suspect adherence to the diet guidelines or a lack of effectiveness of the companion therapy. This approach preys on the multitudes of families still caught up in the "Why" trap. They set up an argument where they cannot lose, and thousands of families are left in a lurch feeling like they aren't doing the biomedical part "right," and if they could only figure it out, their child would improve. Bad science indeed!

The bottom line is this: A handful of relatively inexpensive tests can tell you if you need to embark on the GFCF Diet journey. A lack of evidence in support of the diet as a *general* treatment for ASDs should lead one to seriously question whether the potential reward is worth the effort. If your test results come back positive, you should absolutely consider the Diet an important part of your overall therapy plan – for your child's food allergies. If there are no biomedical indications, it's a huge waste of time, money, and energy to embark on the Diet journey.

False Belief #4: Autism Is Caused By _____

Many of the more popular books on ASDs are written by proponents of biomedical interventions. These can range from diets and massive supplement doses to hormone injections, hyperbaric oxygen chambers, and chelation. In defense of the authors, many of these books were written a decade ago or longer, and much of the research that has debunked a number of their recommended biomedical treatments was done after their books were published. The more recent books on the topic, however, are without excuse. No one can objectively look at the science for many of the common biomedical interventions and claim that they should be universally adopted by all families with a child with an ASD, but much like the TV evangelists who most certainly know their "healings" are a fake, I can only assume they continue spreading their propaganda because they either don't know the science or because it's a great way to make a living. I can forgive celebrities and other parents like me, but it is my sincere hope that the medical professionals who intentionally mislead thousands for self-enrichment will someday have to answer for the damage they have done to countless numbers of families.

I will deal with some of the more common biomedical interventions thoroughly in a later book. In the meantime, however, the way to think about any biomedical intervention is the same way you should think about the GFCF diet: if your child exhibits biomedical indications for their ASD, you should consider the appropriate biomedical intervention. If they have excess mercury in their system, consider chelation. If they have a vitamin deficiency, consider the appropriate supplements. If they have a secretin (or other hormone) deficiency, consider hormone injections. If they have low oxygen levels, maybe a hyperbaric chamber is right for you. If your child does *not* have verifiable biomedical issues, however, in my opinion you should not consider implementing these biomedical interventions. Period.

Unfortunately, you also have to be very careful where you get your child tested and who interprets the test results. The doctors who perform these types of interventions are financially motivated to convince you that you should engage in them. Thus, you should have an independent laboratory do the testing, and should have the results explained to you by a medical professional who is skeptical of biomedical interventions before going to a biomedical professional. At the very least, you will have gotten multiple opinions from varying viewpoints. At best, you may save yourself hundreds of hours and thousands of dollars, plus avoid exposing your child to unnecessary health risks.

The 4 Types of Therapies Every Family Should Consider

In spite of all of the bad science that exists and the number of snake-oil salesmen willing to charge thousands of dollars per month for therapies whose values are dubious at best, there are, fortunately, many therapies that have good, solid research behind them and have been proven effective in nearly all situations. These should make up the core of your efforts towards remediating your child's ASD.

Applied Behavioral Analysis (ABA) Therapies

For most children and adults with an ASD, ABA should be the cornerstone of any intervention program. ABA is a scientifically-rooted class of therapies in which observable baselines are set, therapeutic techniques applied, and the results are tested against the baseline to indicate success or failure – true improvement or the lack thereof. ABA techniques are also often used in observation to determine causes of behavior in order to facilitate better treatments.

ABA has its roots in Behavioral Psychology, which hearkens all the way back to Pavlov and his salivating dog. The basic tenet goes something like this: A behavior (or response) is the result of some antecedent (or stimulus). For Pavlov, he would ring a bell (a stimulus) but the dog would do nothing, since the bell had no meaning associated with it. He would then begin to pair that ringing bell with food (another stimulus), however. The dog would then salivate when the food was presented (a response). After a number of pairings, the dog would salivate when the bell was rung, even when food was not presented. Thus, Pavlov was able to cause the dog to respond to a non-natural stimulus. This is known as "Classical Conditioning."

Later, B.F. Skinner wrote about a different type of behavioral conditioning. In his experiments, instead of pairing a reinforcing stimulus with a non-reinforcing stimulus, he simply waited for a hungry rat to accidentally press a lever. When it did, he gave it a food pellet. Later, Skinner would only reward the rat when a light was turned on, but not when it was off. The rat soon exhibited the desired behavior: when the light was on, it would press the lever, but when the light was off, it would not. This is called "Operant Conditioning," and is aimed at shaping a behavior by reinforcing naturally occurring behaviors rather than directly manipulating a desired behavior by artificial pairings.

Today, there are many different types of ABA that make use of both kinds of conditioning. The most common type is Discrete Trial Therapy (DTT), which teaches almost any skill in very small steps via one-on-one training, repetition, and reinforcement. There are many other ABA therapies, however in the world of Autism, DTT and ABA are often used interchangeably by non-professionals.

While the various ABA therapies vary greatly in approach, they all have certain things in common: the creation of an observed baseline of behavior, the implementation of an intervention designed to produce a desired change in behavior, and comparing behavior after intervention to the baseline in order to test the effectiveness of the intervention. If your child can successfully imitate motor movements (for example, you clap you hands and they can clap theirs if requested), odds are very good that a well-run ABA can facilitate dramatic improvements in your child's life skills.

I will write an in-depth review of the various ABA therapy approaches in my next book, as well as an honest evaluation of the criticisms often levied against it.

Social/Emotional Therapies

Another class of emerging therapies that are based in scientific research and have gained attention is what I call Social/Emotional therapies. The good therapies in this field are based on emerging research in child development, and extrapolated to address deficits in a child with an ASD. Relatively speaking, these ideas are still in their infancy. Proponents of Social/Emotional therapies are still trying to create an empirically sound and universally agreed-upon "Social Development Theory" that they can use as a base for both therapy and research, which is no easy task. In contrast, behavioral therapists had their equivalent in place before ABA was ever conceived.

There are three major Social/Emotional ideas in existence today: Social Thinking, Relationship Development Intervention (RDI), and the Development, Individual-difference, Relationship-based Model (DIR), often referred to as Floortime. Many times these therapies end up being the antithesis of ABA therapies, and they sometimes address the same deficits in very different ways. Because of these differences, quite often ABA therapists are at odds with Social/Emotional therapists, with each claiming the other either does no real good or actually does more harm than good.

This is unfortunate, as I personally believe that: 1) they really aren't always as different as the two sides would have you believe, and 2) they're both very good – just at very different things. For Timothy, we relied on ABA therapies for most of his progress for the first several months, and then slowly integrated Social/Emotional approaches (specifically Relationship Development Intervention, or RDI) into his plan once his functioning had reached an appropriate level to address needs that ABA simply was not designed to address.

Legitimate Biomedical Interventions

Another legitimate approach to treating ASD-related behaviors can be found in the field of modern pharmacology. I am very skeptical about treating ASDs with medicine before other treatments have been applied, and I personally would not advocate for drugs that serve to "zombify" a child (for lack of a better term) unless that were the only viable alternative from a "safety of the child" perspective. That said, one common (though not universal) attribute of Autism is the presence of high levels of anxiety in novel or unpredictable social environments. You can think of it as being like stage fright – only for many with an ASD, the whole world is really their stage. Recently, new drugs have been released that appear to have many of the benefits of other anxiety medications without the dulling side effects. If ABA and Social/Emotional therapies alone aren't enough to help your child deal with their social anxiety after an extended time period, you should consider adding an anti-anxiety medication to your treatment regimen. As of the writing of this book we have *not* done that for Timothy, but are keeping this option open if it appears to be necessary in the coming years.

Other biomedical approaches, like the ones mentioned earlier in the chapter, should be approached skeptically, but not completely ruled out. Again, if your child has independently verifiable deficits that indicate any of the various biomedical approaches will be of benefit, you should consider adding them to your therapy plan.

Speech/Language, Developmental, Physical, and Occupational Therapies

Other traditional therapies are also very effective, depending on the needs of the individual with ASD. If your child has apparent sensory issues, find a good occupational therapist with an ABA background and sensory needs as a specialty. If speech and language are a problem, find a good speech and language therapist with an ABA background, and depending on your child, possibly a specialty in PECS – the Picture Exchange Communications System. Developmental therapy, visual therapy, music therapy, audio integration therapy, and physical therapy may also be appropriate depending on the needs and tendencies of your child.

How to Know Which Therapies are Right for Your Child

One key thing I want to get across yet again is that you should treat only the symptoms that *your* child presents (remember, ASD does not manifest itself in the same way in all who are diagnosed), critically evaluate all treatment options, and do not embark on a therapy route that is not behaviorally or biomedically indicated. Period. I've said it before: don't let unexamined and unreflecting fear guide how you spend your precious time, money, and energy dealing with your child's symptoms. Look at the science, look at your child's specific behaviors, and look at genetic and blood test results administered by an independent laboratory not affiliated with an Autism therapy group.

If your child has behavioral issues, treat them with behavioral therapies. If they have sensory issues, treat them with sensory therapies. If they have biomedical indications, use biomedical therapies. If your child is non-verbal, implement PECS. PECS can also be useful even if the child *is* verbal, but hasn't made the appropriate developmental connections between language and communication. If they have social and emotional issues (and they will), treat them with social/emotional therapies. If, after all that, there appear to be specific anxieties or obsessive-compulsive behaviors that can't be remediated with therapy alone, consider medications to treat the specific symptoms. Don't embark on treatment paths that have significant risks and little evidence indicating that they are going to be of benefit.

This isn't always easy. There are a number of behaviors that may potentially have multiple root causes, even in the same child. For example, a child may have an oral sensory issue that makes them want to naturally put disgusting things in their mouth to get that sensation (the opposite problem that Timothy had as a very young child). After a short time, however, the child may realize that engaging in this behavior garners them lots of attention, and so they may engage in it for reasons that go beyond their sensory needs.

Some kids with ASDs also may have behaviors that could be treated with an ABA therapy, but the root cause may actually be social/emotional, and so addressing that specific behavior will only cause the social/emotional problem to exhibit itself in another way. It's not always easy to tell when you should use one treatment vs. another, and oftentimes we found that multiple approaches to a single behavior were required at the same time to address the multiple causes.

The key is to be patient, to be a careful observer of your child's behavior, and when you're not sure what to do, experiment with different things that might be appropriate and see what happens. Take good data, and make sure you're getting objective feedback from that data to indicate whether or not your approach is working. Attack each symptom from as much of a scientific approach as possible, and be aware that the approach that worked yesterday may not effectively treat the same symptom tomorrow. As your child evolves through their ASD, evolve their treatment to keep up with them, and never stop pushing them towards higher and higher levels of functioning. It is my firm belief that having high expectations is an important key to achieving a favorable outcome.

An excellent resource for sifting through the mountain of information that's out there on ASDs is the Autism Watch site: http://www.autism-watch.org. This site focuses on a scientific approach to autism, diagnosis, and treatments. Because of their objective and science-based approach, I strongly recommend exploring it and following their recommendations.

The #1 Reason Kids with Autism Don't Make Progress

Mrs. Keller, I don't think Helen's greatest handicap is deafness or blindness. I think it's your love and pity.
—*Anne Bancroft as Annie Sullivan in "The Miracle Worker" (1962)*

One of the dangers of loving a child with an ASD is the propensity to want to make them happy or comfortable – after all, it's not their fault they have the disorder. Life is probably not going to be fair for them over the long haul, and things are going to be harder than they are for most people. Unfortunately, this leads many, many parents and other family members to engage in practices that are detrimental to the child's progress.

Any time you allow a negative behavior from a child with an ASD that you would not allow in a typically developing child, you have unconsciously enabled and reinforced that behavior. If you continue to engage in and reinforce these behaviors, you are creating a world without accountability for the child, and they will not be motivated to do the hard work of recovery because their incentives are misaligned.

The following example may make me appear an unsympathetic person, but it illustrates the point very well. After several months of Timothy's treatment, we were experiencing some great progress, but we noticed that with certain people that his negative behaviors would shoot through the roof. We watched and realized that the problem was that they were enabling and excusing behaviors they would not have allowed in a typically developing child because of his diagnosis. One night a family member who I will call "Aunt Susan" was sitting at our dinner table helping Timothy eat, and he did something he knew was not permitted. I immediately addressed the situation, holding firm the line that he had to do what was expected before he could go play. Aunt Susan, in front of all of us, came to his defense stating that he was just tired and would probably do better next time if he could just get down and play. I immediately recognized this as a pivotal moment.

Timothy's Aunt Susan loves him very much, so much that it's hard for them to see him suffer from being told he can't do something he wants to do. In a typically developing kid, you call that "spoiling" and it's not all bad. Nearly all grandparents, godparents, aunts, and uncles I know do it! Unfortunately, in the case of a child with an ASD, the stakes are much, much higher, and the negative outcomes can be infinitely worse. We had already talked to Aunt Susan numerous times about the need to be consistent in our expectations, but these "good cop" talks were simply not working – the interference had continued unabated. I had to address both his behavior and Aunt Susan's behavior.

I replied by looking at Timothy, but saying in front of everyone, "Well Timothy, it looks like [Aunt Susan] wants you to have the Autism." You can imagine the response – it was as though I had slapped her in the face. It and the ensuing conversation did, however, finally get the point across – she was not loving him with her behavior; she was enabling him in ways that would prove extremely harmful as he got older, and I was now going to start calling her on it.

As terrible as I'm sure I come across here, the story has a happy ending. After the initial shock of my statement wore off, we had another in-depth conversation about our strategies and the problems deviating from them would cause. I can't say that Aunt Susan started toeing the line in the same way we did, but she did get noticeably better. More importantly, though, she stopped interfering when we stepped in to make him act appropriately (for the most part). That was a big victory that has continued to make a significant difference in Timothy's life.

One other note about tough love: I think sometimes people confuse self-love with love for their children. If you're not willing to put your child through a rigorous therapy regimen with the requisite discipline and uncomfortable moments, is it because you love the child too much, **or is it because you love yourself too much** to put yourself through that particular inconvenience or pain? There's probably a combination of factors, but let's be very clear and define what love really is: love for a child with an ASD is doing whatever is necessary to give them the best possible life, regardless of how hard it is on you or the child in the short-term. Thus, true love may make your child cry, may cause them to miss a snack and go hungry for a short time, may make them lose toys, and may make you feel like a cold-hearted S.O.B. This may be the most important statement in this book: PLEASE love your child enough to put them (and you!) through the necessary pain in the short term so that they'll have a better life in the long term.

I fully believe it is one of the most important keys to Timothy's amazing and continuing recovery. You have to be strong, and that means putting your child through paces that they won't immediately understand and that don't seem fair for a kid their age. To the best of your ability, put your pity on the shelf. It will be incredibly hard, but one day when your child can look at you and with full emotion tell you they love you and give you a hug as you're putting them to bed, it will be worth it all. Trust me.

Chapter 3: How to Navigate Legal and Political Issues

The vast majority of the folks you will deal with got into their respective fields because they really love kids with special needs. That does not, unfortunately, mean that they are always able to do what is best for you and your child, nor are they able to freely and fully disclose all of the information you need in order to make the best decisions. Learning how to navigate "the system" was one of the more painful elements of our journey. This section is designed to help you understand why those who love and care for your children may not necessarily be acting in your best interests, despite what they might want to do, and how you can deal with it.

The Top 3 Mistakes People Make When Dealing With School Systems and Government Agencies

Believing That They All Share the Same Goals as You Do

If most people got into this field because they love kids, then why might they not be as helpful as possible? In many cases it all comes down to funding. Here's an example of why this might be the default behavior:

Let's say a certain school district invests heavily in programs to support kids that are severely affected with ASDs, and there are no information restrictions in place. It quickly becomes common knowledge in the entire ASD community that this school district is the absolute best place to be. Kids are improving left and right, teaching quality is high, and outcomes are measurably better than in any other school district in the area. What might be the natural outcomes? First of all, almost every parent who had a child with an ASD would want to be there. This might cause several things to happen:

1) Housing prices in that district could skyrocket due to increased competition for the school from families with an ASD-affected child.
   a. Only families that could afford the homes could get into the district
   b. This would in effect deny services to those with lesser financial means
2) The proportion of affected vs. non-affected children would skew sharply compared to surrounding districts.
   a. The sharp increase in the number of ASD-affected kids would pressure the school's resources, most likely beyond capacity
   b. The quality of the services would drop as finite resources were spread over a larger number of ASD-affected kids
3) Parents in other school districts would compare available services and would protest the lack of services in their district compared to the "good" one
   a. Schools already struggling to operate would be put in the position of having to provide some semblance of the same services or face lawsuits
   b. Money that would have otherwise been allocated to teacher raises, school improvements, additional programs, community outreach, etc., would be redirected to ASD programs
   c. The newly affected groups would now protest, and a dizzying spiral would ensue where the school district simply could not win
4) Taxes would have to be increased in order to pay for everything that was needed for every child
   a. Special interest groups would almost certainly protest the higher taxes, demand more accountability, and threaten to "throw the bums out" if they couldn't manage their budgets better
   b. If they succeeded, the new management's first obvious cut would be in the area of special-needs programming, since

       it is so much higher per child than other programs and other districts

    c. All the work done to build special-needs programs might be lost, or diluted to the point of ineffectiveness

Let's face it: every dollar a school district spends on an ASD-related program is a dollar that cannot be spent improving playgrounds, giving well-deserved raises to teachers, or making schools safer and more effective for the other 99% of the school population. ASD programs are disproportionately expensive to operate. Thus school districts are put in a tight spot.

The same goes for state and local government agencies. The resources of a state are finite, but the need for services is extremely high. Government agencies that provide good services might find a disproportionate number of families moving into their jurisdiction to get access to them. As finite resources get spread over more and more disproportionate numbers of ASD-affected kids, services (and corresponding payments for those services) would have to be cut in order to meet the ever growing need. Again, the same spiral could ensue, but on an even larger scale.

I get it; I really do. If you're a government agency or a school district trying to manage a seemingly infinite need on a finite budget, I imagine you have to make some tough calls and set up some roadblocks to keep from becoming completely ineffective for those you are able to serve. You'd explain this damaging spiral to your people and train your employees and those who work for you not to say too much or give specific (and costly) advice. You could threaten them with a loss of income if they overstepped by limiting the number of paying contracts, or even a loss of license to practice in your jurisdiction – you might even set up legal obstacles to sharing information. You'd be doing it so you could protect your programs and provide the best possible treatment for the kids you served (or at least the legally-required minimum level of treatment), in part by limiting the numbers of kids you served.

It's logical. It makes sense. I might even do the same thing if I were in their shoes. But as a parent of an ASD-affected child, I couldn't care less.

Failure to Prepare for a Fight

My point in explaining this is *not* to make you sympathize with the other side or accept lesser levels of services in an effort to achieve some unknown "greater good." My point here is simply to make you aware of one of the potential frames of reference under which those who serve you and your child may be operating. Their rational responsibility is to protect the overall system, and that unfortunately forces them to try to limit services in some cases. Most of these people aren't evil – in fact, most have good intentions. They *can't* be open founts of information lest they risk the effectiveness or financial stability of their programs and, as such, you must understand that every piece of information you get is going to be tainted. Your rational responsibility is to make sure that your child has every opportunity and all of the services he or she needs for success.

Not everyone you deal with will have good intentions – although many will. Some of the more bureaucratic types who have allowed career progression to cloud their original desire to care for children will exploit their knowledge and your ignorance to the greatest degree possible. It is up to you to figure out how to navigate an environment where those you depend on for care and treatment are really *not* what they may seem to be, an environment where seemingly innocent conversations and suggestions can have severely detrimental effects on your child's recovery in the name of saving money. Do not be fooled – it's a jungle out there.

The good news is that legally you are in a very, very good position. Missouri, for instance, decrees by law that every child must receive the educational support they need, regardless of the cost. The same goes for government agencies, which are not allowed to deny services if a child qualifies and a parent requests them. The tricky part is figuring out what roadblocks the agencies and school districts may choose to employ in order to keep the flow of information as low as possible.

3 Common Tactics Employed Against Parents

Here are three of the more common tactics we've run into in Timothy's journey:

1) Don't Ask, Don't Tell: This is by far the most common tactic employed, to my knowledge. While school districts and government agencies cannot refuse services for which you qualify, they are not necessarily obligated to provide services that you do not specifically request. This is especially damaging for new parents on the journey, as they are still severely emotionally distraught and may not know their rights and options, and may waste precious time early on employing sub-optimal strategies. The solution for this tactic is education, and this book and others like it are important resources in that process.

2) Panel of Experts: Agencies and districts decree that "the team" must make decisions for the child, not just the parents. As such, they stack IFSPs and IEPs (Individualized Education Program meetings held by school districts) with their own employees whose first obligations are to the school or agency. If the entire team agrees except for the parents, then a decision can be made against parent wishes. The solution for this tactic is to level the playing field by *always* bringing your own trusted advocates and experts to these meetings (which usually means you're paying for their time). If you have at least one expert on either side of the table that agrees with you and dissents against what the overall team is proposing, you have a much better shot at getting what your child *really* needs if you find yourself in a defensive position.

3) We Don't Offer That Here: Another common tactic – sure, your child demonstrably may need 10+ hours per week of one-on-one ABA therapy (which you may have to prove by paying for it at home for a few months and tracking the results), but your school district doesn't offer it, so it's a moot point. The only problem for the school is that this particular stance is illegal in many states. The solution here is to educate yourself about the education laws in your state and be willing to stand up for your legal rights. This is usually a bluff, and possibly a delay tactic on their part. If they're

35

smart, they know that if you take the matter to court, you will probably win. Don't be afraid to bring this to their attention. Therapy is expensive, but lawsuits can be much, much more expensive. Keep in mind though, this will be true for you as well.

Fighting When It's Not Necessary or Helpful

This is all well and good, but you do need to approach this with a strong dose of realistic expectations. The reality is that in many schools across the country, particularly those in smaller communities and rural areas, special education services are very limited for children with an ASD. Many schools do not have full blown ABA programs, or an array of special services for these children. Many schools do not have on-staff OTs and PTs, and may only have one or two speech pathologists to service all the members of their student population who need such help.

If you find yourself in this situation – your school has very little to offer and you have no alternatives available – it is of course a battle worth fighting. However, your child needs full-blown services now, not in a year or two or three, or however long it would take for a lawsuit to make it worthwhile for the district to put a more complete set of services in place. It is often not financially feasible for a small town school district to invest the thousands upon thousands of dollars for an ABA program for a very small handful of students. It does, however, make sense for large school districts in metropolitan areas to do so. A school in a metro area may find themselves with 50 or more kids with Autism, rather than the five or less that a small town school may have. It is an unfortunate truth, but not all schools are able to adequately and equally provide services for a child with Autism.

If that is your reality, you have a decision to make. We did not have the time, money, or energy to fight an uphill battle with a school district; we were already busy at home fighting an uphill battle with Timothy. We did our research (not all metropolitan area schools are created equally either) and then moved to a district that had a solid ABA program in place. This had not always been the case for this district. Several years prior, other families had taken the time and spent resources to file lawsuits because of inadequate services, and over a few years time a strong ABA program had been put into place. At the time, there likely were no other established ABA programs in the area, so someone had to pave the way. In our case, we decided it was best for our family to move to an area where such programs were already in place. We would have moved to a different state, changed jobs, or done whatever was necessary to get Timothy the best therapy and support possible.

3 Indicators of a Good School District

We were deeply committed to being in a good school district. We asked various therapists (as well as other parents we had met at TouchPoint) for information about different school districts in the area. Although many of the therapists danced around the issue, we got around it by asking questions about the areas rather than the schools, by asking about research strategies rather than specific recommendations, and by giving scenarios and letting therapists fill in the blanks.

1. We learned that, generally speaking, if you have two side-by-side school districts, one of which has a noticeably higher price per square foot in the homes that were for sale than the other, chances were good that the higher-priced homes were located in an area that has better services.

2. We learned that it was critically important to take tours of early childhood centers and preschools to get a feel for their quality, and that the quality of a building would sometimes also reflect the quality of services available. We also learned that during the tour you should directly ask about services for kids on the Autism spectrum, and that the specificity and forthrightness of the responses would be indicative of how good those services might actually be. For example, if the answers were vague and danced around "tailored to the individual needs of the child," they might

not have the kinds of programs in place to support kids with Autism.

3. Another suggested investigation tool was to search for information about the financial status of a school district, as well as what school districts spend on a per-student basis. The better the finances and the greater the per-child spending, the more likely that services could be provided. In Missouri, most of this information can be found on the Internet, often on the school's own Web site.

These suggestions were not given to us as absolutes, but guidelines we formulated to indicate that further investigation was warranted. For our own search, we had already talked to other parents who had given us suggestions for school districts, and we researched, dug in, and asked questions until we had a list of four really good districts to further evaluate. We quickly realized that our current school district was not desirable, but one preschool with a great reputation, relatively higher home prices per square foot, and a modern and well-kept early childhood center with specific Autism programs (including ABA classrooms), and strong financials was located near the private school that our daughter Emily was attending. This helped make our decision a little easier.

8 Things Every Parent *Must* Do To Prepare

There are several general principles that you must follow if you are going to navigate your particular government or school system as effectively as possible. Again, while most of the people you work with have good intentions, they work in a system in which they may not always be able to do what is best for your child unless you advocate for it in the right way. An incomplete list of necessary skills follows:

1. <u>Learn the language of the system</u>: "I'm interested in XYZ therapy" does not mean the same thing as "I want my child evaluated for XYZ therapy." If you're not sure what language you should use,

try asking "What would I need to say in order to get my child evaluated for XYZ?" If they try to dodge the question or delay answering, firmly but politely repeat the question, and then when they tell you, say that phrase. It feels like an unnecessary exercise, and it really should be, but unfortunately you may have to learn how to play the legal language games they live by.

2. Understand the legal power of your position as a parent with an ASD-affected child: In many states, you have a right to call an IEP or IFSP at any time and have your child's progress re-evaluated and therapy regimen adjusted to meet their current status. If you're being dismissed by the school or agency, the phrase "due process" (law suit) is the nuclear option you have at your disposal in the event of a stalemate. You shouldn't use it lightly or often, but be willing to pull it out if you have to in order to get your child's needs met. As long as you're being reasonable, the law is most definitely on your side. Again, though, this is an expensive and time-consuming process. Only use this as a last resort.

3. Learn how to ask questions: When you find a therapist who really cares about your family and you have developed a strong relationship with them, you can phrase questions in such a way that answering them will give you the information you need without risking their jobs or opening them up to liability. This is a delicate balance, but one that can be navigated if you're careful.

4. Learn to be blunt: This is really hard, but absolutely necessary if you are facing a service provider that you feel is playing games. For example, you must be willing to ask "Is this a matter of what my child needs, or a funding issue? If it's a funding issue, let's talk about it in those terms." If it legally cannot be a funding issue, then you've framed the discussion in such a way that they have to explain why you shouldn't receive a service rather than you having to explain why they are needed. If you feel a teacher or therapist has ulterior motives in stating that your child doesn't need certain services, you should call that out directly and in the meeting. Again, this is uncomfortable, but will turn the tables neatly on a group that may be trying to play games with your child's future.

5. Do whatever it takes to educate yourself about reputable available treatments and your state's obligations to provide them: This book is a great start, but you need a lot more in order to be fully

equipped with all of your options. Some way, somehow, you must come up to speed – and quickly. Personally, I strongly recommend the TouchPoint Autism Services Parent Training Program. It made such a huge difference for us that I will dedicate a whole chapter to this extremely valuable two-week program.

6. Stack the deck in your favor: Build a multi-dimensional and cross-functional team of experts with different backgrounds and experiences, and exploit each one of them (in a good way) for what they bring to the table. Bring your administrative experts and other experts to your IEPs and IFSPs, and pay them for their time. It's expensive, but much less expensive than being overrun or being taken advantage of because you didn't have the right people there. In another chapter, we will discuss the various personalities that have helped us through our journey thus far, and I strongly recommend that you find as wide and deep of a team as possible to enable your success. Some groups even offer advocacy programs at no cost, but never take on an advocate you don't know and who doesn't know your situation and strategy. Make sure you have a tight-knit team, and that all members know what is going on and what their role is in taking the next steps.

7. Develop and stick to a strategy: Along with keeping the team apprised of current situations and status, you must at all times have a clearly developed strategy. This includes pulling your team together *before* an IEP or IFSP and going over what you are going to propose and how you are going to justify it. Don't be fooled – the other side is likely doing the same thing. You must have a clearly defined set of goals and reasons for the measures you are seeking and a proposed solution for how to obtain them before walking into a meeting, or else you will be severely disadvantaged when it comes time to talk about what to do next with your child.

8. Be prepared to fight tooth and nail – but fight fair: Never walk away from an IEP or IFSP without being satisfied with the end result, unless you are walking away to reconvene at a later date. At the same time, make sure that the thing you are advocating for is end results, not the means to those results. For example, if a school doesn't have an ABA-supported classroom environment that you feel your child needs but is willing to provide a special-ed environment with an ABA shadow, that might be an equivalent

solution, depending on the needs of your child. Maybe a social group twice per week really would accomplish the same thing as two sessions of developmental therapy per week – again, depending on the specific needs of your child. Work with the other side to the furthest extent possible. Most of them really do love kids, and it's not their fault that their hands are tied. Creative solutions can usually be found if a group thinks about them long and hard enough – at least in our experience. Do your best to be friendly during, before, and after meetings. Just make sure during the meeting that you don't settle for less than what your child really, demonstrably needs.

Employing these principles may mean there are times when you walk out of meetings without an agreement. You *must* be willing to do so. (We did more than once.) You may have to delay meetings in order to assemble your team and get them up to speed – don't be afraid to exercise your right to do so, reminding the other side that if they call a meeting without you, that you will simply reconvene another one later and undo whatever has been done if necessary. (Fortunately, we never had to do this, but had that option ready.) You may have to refuse to allow a meeting that you think is a set-up where necessary services are going to try to be cut, and be willing to do so in writing, with strong language, on both legal and ethical grounds. (We did that, too.) It will cost you money for good therapists to give time to your strategy sessions and meetings. If you don't have unlimited funds, it's never easy to pay those bills when they're not going directly towards therapy time for your child. You must understand, however, that this is a highly-leveraged investment that is absolutely as important as anything they might do directly with your child, if not more so. Do what you have to do to pay those bills.

It is never easy or pleasant to knowingly enter into a conflict, but your child is worth it. In the end, if you are reasonable, play fair, and refuse to take things personally, you can maintain positive relationships with those who are helping your child along their route to recovery – or at least the ones with whom you care to maintain a positive relationship. Most of the people we have dealt with fall into that category.

Jason D. Eden, M.B.A.

How to Deal with the Rest of the World

Understand Your Rights in Neighborhood and Housing Disputes

In addition to learning how to navigate schools and government agencies, you may find yourself having to navigate a different world in terms of neighborhoods and housing as well. One of the accommodations we made in order to fund Timothy's therapy was to downscale our living arrangement plans, but to do so in the right school district for Timothy's preschool. We found ourselves moving out of our house, renting it out, and renting a unit on the 4th floor of a condo near the early childhood center we had identified as Timothy's best option. It was definitely a painful "learning experience" for us in many ways, and forced us to employ the principles above that we were using in other environments for the same basic reasons.

As with schools and government agencies, it's important that you understand your rights. One of the most important things to be aware of in U.S. law is the Fair Housing Act. The full text can be found here:

http://www.justice.gov/crt/housing/title8.php

It's a long read, full of lots of legalese, but critical knowledge to have on hand should the need arise to use it. In a nutshell, the act dictates that neighborhood associations, condo associations, landlords, real estate agents, home sellers, and other housing providers by law can *not* discriminate against your family in any way because you have a child with a disability. They cannot deny you housing, access to services available to others, or impose special fees. You also have the right to seek reasonable accommodations that would be required in order for your child to have equal access to what is available to everyone else, although some of them may be at your own expense. Basically, you have the right to be treated like any other human being, and to ask for reasonable accommodations to enable your child's full access to neighborhood services.

3 Common Mistakes to Avoid In Housing Situations

I wish that were enough, but unfortunately, we live in a world where motives are not always pure. As such, it is important that you not only understand your rights, but that you play the game smartly – anticipate the moves that the other side might make, and counter appropriately for your child's best advantage. It's unfortunate that this is required, but it is true. Here are some basic suggestions for navigating housing issues:

1. <u>Don't mention it</u>. When you're looking at housing options, you are not required to disclose anything other than in certain cases the number of people that will be living in the place at which you are looking. Frankly, if the person showing you the property notices that you have a special-needs child and they don't want to go further with you, they can make up 100 different excuses as to why, and it would be difficult if not impossible to prove discrimination. Thus, when looking at housing options, *don't bring your child with you*. Find a babysitter, family member, or service, but do not give the person you are dealing with any indication that you have a special-needs child. What do you have to gain? Nothing. You have a lot to lose. Also, if you're a talker by nature, make sure you practice what you're willing to say before you go out and don't say anything about your child.

2. <u>Don't (completely) trust a salesperson</u>: A real estate salesperson has one job – to sell or lease you a property and bring home a commission. While they cannot lie about a property, they can carefully phrase things in a way that misleads without subjecting themselves to legal liability. Thus, be sure to look around a neighborhood in addition to the actual property you are interested in. Are there other kids in the neighborhood? If not, that could indicate that kids in general are unwelcome, and you are likely to experience conflict with the neighbors when it comes to your special-needs child. You may still decide that the place is right, but you'll need to be fully armed, know your rights, and be ready for some fights.

3. <u>When you have to fight, do it in writing</u>: If you have an unfortunate face-to-face conversation with someone, write it down to the best of your ability, then summarize the main ideas and deliver a copy of the letter to the person you spoke with, the association president (if applicable), your landlord (if applicable), and your lawyer (if you have one). Invite the other party to respond and correct any misunderstandings, and get a dialogue going if possible. It's better, however, if you can initiate a conversation in email or written form, and have this written communication log from the beginning. If someone publishes something discriminatory in a newsletter, save a copy, write a reply to the author (and the other folks mentioned above), and again, keep everything. If you *do* have to threaten a lawsuit, these written records can serve as evidence of a pattern of discrimination that will bolster your case. If you're lucky, they'll be enough to stop the discriminatory behavior without ever filing a lawsuit.

How to Take Time Off of Work for Therapy or Training

One of the struggles when you get a diagnosis for your child is figuring out how to balance the significant time demands that these new circumstances in your life will require. You are going to need time off from work to get yourself trained in how to effectively treat your child, get them evaluated, and potentially perform therapy yourself while you're building up a team. If you don't have or don't want to take vacation time to do all of this, there are still options for taking the necessary time without risking the loss of your job. At the federal level in the U.S., the main thing you need to be aware of is the Family and Medical Leave Act (FMLA).

Basically, the FMLA states that an employer must give you up to 12 workweeks of unpaid leave during any 12-month period to "care for a family member with a serious health condition." While the leave *is* unpaid in most states and companies, it does give you the option to do things like attend seminars and trainings (such as TouchPoint's Parent Training Program) without using vacation time and without the risk of retaliation or job loss. You are also usually able to take FMLA time in small chunks if you need to – for example, if you would like to work 30 hours per week so that you can perform 10 hours of therapy per week with your child while you are recruiting a therapy team, you can do that and use 10 hours per week of FMLA time until you have exhausted the equivalent of 12 full workweeks per calendar year. You just have to keep good documentation showing that you are actually using the time for treatment and care.

The key here is to get in touch with your company's Human Resources department to discuss your options and intentions as early as possible. There are certain rules that apply for using FMLA time, and very small companies may not be subject to the requirements. Many states have guidelines that go beyond what FMLA requires as well, and may have different requirements for what constitutes a "covered employer." Educate yourself about the FMLA and the equivalent options in your state (or country, if you're not in the U.S.), get in touch with HR, and if you can afford it and need the time, take it in order to further your child's recovery.

2 Commonly Overlooked Options for Funding Therapy Expenses

Building and maintaining an intense early intervention program can be expensive. One of the ways to help offset some of these expenses in the U.S. is by utilizing Flexible Spending Accounts, (FSAs) if your workplace offers them as a benefit. An FSA allows you to have pre-tax dollars taken out of your paycheck. That money can then be used to pay for eligible expenses, which increases the amount of money you have available for therapy and other medical expenses because those dollars are taken out pre-tax.

At the time of this writing, there were generally two types of FSAs: Dependent Day Care Reimbursement Accounts and Health Care Reimbursement Accounts (HCRAs). HCRA money can be used to pay for any *bona fide* therapy, including those not covered by insurance. Plans vary widely on coverage for occupational, physical, speech/language, and developmental therapy, so check with your insurance provider to see what is available. Another huge benefit of HCRAs (especially compared to other types of FSA accounts) is that you can withdraw from them before you have actually contributed and accrued the necessary funds. For example, if you elected to contribute $5,000 to an HCRA and had a $5,000 expense in the first month of the year, you can claim the entire reimbursement before you have contributed the full $5,000 to that amount. Thus, not only do you get the tax benefit, but it's also essentially an interest-free loan.

Drawbacks to FSAs: Flexible Spending Accounts have limits as to the amount you can contribute. They are also "use it or lose it" plans, meaning any money left in your account at the end of the plan year goes back to your employer and is lost to you forever. Thus, it is important that you carefully plan ahead. Again, I strongly recommend that you get engaged with your HR and/or Benefits department to discuss your options regarding these types of accounts.

If you are self-employed or self-insured in the U.S., under certain conditions you have the option of opening a Health Savings Account (HSA). As with an HCRA, HSA money can be used to pay for qualified health care and therapy expenses on a pre-tax basis. One significant catch is that you cannot contribute to an HSA unless your insurance policy is a "High Deductible Health Plan" (HDHP). In 2008, a HDHP was defined as one that had a family deductible of $2,200, with an annual out-of-pocket limit of $11,200. The idea is that these insurance policies are less expensive, so the premium savings can be contributed to the HSA. If most of the therapies your child needs are not covered by insurance, an HSA might be an excellent way to reduce your overall cost of services. HSAs are commonly offered by banks, credit unions, and insurance companies.

These may also be offered by an employer as a benefit, or as an alternative to a traditional low-deductible insurance plan.

Drawbacks to HSAs: as with FSAs, HSAs have limits on contributions. You have to weigh the tax savings compared to the financial risk of only carrying an HDHP health insurance plan. If you have several children or if you or your spouse has chronic health issues, the tax benefit may be outweighed by other medical costs incurred. Like a lot of tax-preferred accounts, these plans have lots of rules, so you will need to educate yourself. You can get started at this web site: https://treas.gov/offices/public-affairs/hsa/faq.shtml. Be sure to ask your HSA provider lots of questions so you can decide if this is right for you.

How To Avoid Getting Scammed

I've said this before, but it bears repeating: just because a person is a medical doctor specializing in Autism does *not* make them a good, honest person. This should *especially* be at the top of your mind if you are thinking of going to a doctor who is not covered by your insurance and will be charging you hundreds of dollars for an initial visit. Odds are, they're primarily interested in finding a sucker who will pay hundreds of dollars for strange sounding "miracle" cures without knowing what they're going to be getting. They probably know that they are not really helping your child. They pair their quack therapies with good ones like ABA and then tell you that the quackery is what is primarily responsible for your child's progress. They tell anecdotes and stories, recruit celebrities, have parents write books, and claim thousands of cures, but can't point to any good, double-blind research to back up their claims, and will intentionally ignore or try to discredit the double-blind research that debunks their methodologies.

You have to think critically, and defend yourself against the onslaught of bad information that's out there and the well-educated pickpockets whose main motivation is to make a buck. If you find a doctor you think is convincing, but the treatment seems a little odd or unusually expensive, get a second opinion from a doctor that does *not* buy into that therapy and listen to both sides. Be careful, follow the science, and don't be a sucker. At the same time, if you've already been victimized, don't feel bad. You're not alone. They've preyed on your love for your child for their personal gain. Be angry, and by all means, if you are currently in their "care," get a second opinion as quickly as you can.

How To Deal With Family and Friends

It is absolutely critical that you keep any friend or family member that will be in consistent contact with your child up to date on progress, strategies that are being employed, the rationale behind them, and what your goals are. It is also very important that you provide support for them if they are going to be watching your child for you. Friends and family members may naturally be more inclined to try to make the child happy than to work with you on achieving your goals, and you must thus make it clear what the consequences will be for the child if that attitude affects their behavior. It may also require you to establish guidelines for visitations that, if not followed, will result in a temporary loss of the right to visit.

Your friends and family have to understand that your child's temporary discomfort or frustration is a small price to pay for what could be years (or even a lifetime) of inappropriate behavior caused by reinforcing the wrong behaviors. It won't always seem fair and you may come across as "the bad guy," but remember your priorities. In my list, the only relationships that came before Timothy's recovery were my wife, my kids, and God. If I had to make a family member upset with me in order to ensure that they would not derail any aspect of Timothy's recovery, I was willing to accept those consequences. Know your priorities, keep your friends and family circle informed, and make them stick to *your* guns to the extent possible. Long term, they'll be an important resource in the recovery process if you're able to train them and enlist their aid in doing things properly.

These can be difficult conversations to have and even harder guidelines to enforce, but if you choose *not* to do so, you may very well be harming your child's level of potential success and happiness for the rest of their life because you refuse to temporarily upset your family or friends. Lean on that priorities list and do the right thing, even if it hurts. It's worth it.

Chapter 4: Two Weeks That Can Change Your Life

The most important thing you can do to impact your child's emergence from an ASD is to change your own thinking sets and behavior patterns. Lots of parents do not know how to follow through on the things therapists are doing with their children. They don't understand the methodologies or goals, and they don't build the same structures into their child's non-therapy time that they have during therapy. In many ways, they end up sabotaging the gains made in therapy on a daily basis. If you can avoid this, you are way ahead of most families.

The rest of this chapter details the TouchPoint Center for Autism's Parent Training Program, which we went through a few months after receiving Timothy's diagnosis. Why spend a whole chapter on a program that only lasts two weeks?

Let's take a quick look at Timothy before we started:

- He was using fewer than one communicative word per day, usually resorting to a meaningless repetitive phrase which we had to guess the meaning of each time. Getting a word out of him, such as "more," took a lot of effort.
- Meaningful eye contact was virtually non-existent.
- He was frequently engaging in self-injurious behaviors. Eye-poking was particularly bad when in the car, to the point that we were afraid he was going to permanently injure his vision. He also engaged in banging his head against people and walls, as well as putting himself in dangerous positions (climbing on top of couches and chairs, etc.).

- He had problems biting, punching, and kicking his sister and us when he was frustrated, and this spilled over into other environments with other children and childcare workers.
- He had extreme, seemingly uncontrollable obsessive-compulsive behaviors. We couldn't go into a building without Timothy finding a wall with lines and pacing back and forth against it. We took rare meals out at non-peak times and would just let him pace while the rest of us ate.

By the end of the program:

- Timothy was using multiple words to communicate needs or respond to questions, sometimes even initiating communication. In two 20-minute sessions on the last day of the Parent Training Program, Timothy used words to communicate 87 times per session, once using more than 40 unique words and phrases!
- Aggressive and self-injurious behaviors were significantly reduced – hitting, kicking, head banging, eye poking, etc.
- Timothy had significant improvements in eye contact, with purposeful eye contact being recorded between 3-5 times per 20-minute therapy session by the end of the program.
- We could go to a restaurant and keep him in his chair. We could go for a walk in the neighborhood. We could take him to a store.

None of these achievements seem significant today, but at the time this list represented an incredible and dramatic improvement in the quality of our lives and our ability to communicate with our child.

Timothy did not have any speech, OT, or DT during that time due to the all-day nature of the TouchPoint program. It is safe to say that all improvements in Timothy were due solely to TouchPoint's methods and therapists, as well as our relentless follow-through. This was clearly a major turning point for our family.

What the Program Does for Parents

The TouchPoint Parent Training Program is an accelerated 2-week program designed to educate parents on a myriad of issues they will face by having a child on the spectrum, plus a very hands-on, practical training program for how to perform an effective type of ABA therapy. Almost everything they do is based on the principles of ABA and is helpful for anyone, regardless of where you are on your Autism journey, but particularly useful if you are early in the process.

> *Note*: The program is constantly being tweaked in order to improve its effectiveness. The program I am describing below is accurate as of this printing, but changes may occur based on research and improvements in results. The program described below is actually greatly improved compared to the same program we attended in 2006, and I suspect that they will continue to be further modified as time goes on. Consult with TouchPoint for specifics on how their program may differ based on what you read below.

The 10 days you spend at TouchPoint while in the program are each formulated in roughly the same fashion: three 20-minute therapy sessions with your child (morning, around lunchtime, and late afternoon) interspersed with information-packed teaching sessions that are generally taught by the actual therapists that are working with you and your child.

The therapy sessions – 30 in all over the 10 days – begin with a baseline where you are recorded working with your child for 20 minutes. The next several sessions are led by your assigned therapist, with you observing the session from behind a one-way mirror or via a digital video feed. Depending on how things progress, usually sometime on the third day, a parent begins sitting in on the therapy sessions with the therapists. As quickly as is feasible, the therapist stops attending the sessions, and from that point on remotely coaches you for the rest of the sessions from behind the mirror or while watching the digital image via a wireless microphone you are wearing. In all, you will usually engage in more than 20 coached therapy sessions over the two weeks, giving you a solid foundation that you can take back home and apply directly after the program.

8 Critical Things the TouchPoint Parent Training Program Teaches

The training sessions are a whirlwind ride that take you from a starting point of knowing nothing about ASDs, and ends up with you being fully-armed to engage the Autism world with your child. TouchPoint spends time orienting you to the program, usually even bringing in a parent who has gone through the program in the past to help provide a different perspective. They start with the basics of ASDs, and quickly move into helping you develop plans and goals for your child right from day one. At a *very* high level, the program will teach you:

- How to change *your* behavior so that you can consistently engage with your child in positive interactions that will help reinforce the behaviors you want to see, rather than unconsciously rewarding negative behaviors
- How to identify reinforcers for your child and explain how to use them effectively in a therapy setting
- The importance of taking good data on your child's behavior and creating baselines, and how to record data in a way that makes sense both to parents and educators
- How to evaluate the functions of behavior through this data so that you can address it and effectively modify it
- The science behind ABA and how to apply and infuse it productively in your own home and educational environments
- Numerous other strategies and treatments, and help you understand how to critically evaluate them
- Common issues for individuals with an ASD, including communication, frustration, anxiety, social skills, etc. and how to address them to meet your child's specific needs
- What supports exist for parents with a child with an ASD, how to access services, and where to go to get support when necessary

All of this is interspersed with direct, hands-on labs and exercises that sometimes use actual clinical tools to produce reports that you can take home and show to therapists and educators in order to save time getting them up to speed on your child's status. Throughout the program you are constantly reviewing the therapy sessions, taking data, and discussing results with the therapists. The in-class discussions are highly-charged environments where parents get to bring their real-world issues to the table, discuss them openly, and strategize with other parents in addition to the therapists for how to deal with your individual situation – be it with your child, your family, your school district, or some other entity. Trust me – this is a jam-packed 10 days!

3 Critical Steps To Ensure the Best Possible Result

If you do extensive research, you will find many parents who claim that TouchPoint is a waste of time. I do not doubt this is true for them, but I believe such an outcome is avoidable for *every* family who goes through the program. When we went through the program, there were three other families that were trained at the same time. Timothy had the greatest recovery experience by far compared to the other kids in his class at the time. While part of this can be attributed to Timothy being ready for a rocket launch, I firmly believe there were other forces at play that contributed greatly to our success with the program. This section will help explain why I think we had such a great experience, and why other families who probably *should* have did not.

Get the Whole Team On Board

Both Melynda and I attended the entire Parent Training Program. We both took off work, arranged childcare for our older daughter when it was required, and frankly did anything that was necessary to ensure that we were both present, engaged, and active during the entire learning process. This is critical because a spouse or significant other who does not attend the training program with you may not understand why you are wanting to make the life changes you will have to make, and may therefore consciously or unconsciously sabotage your efforts because they don't fully understand what you are doing.

This paragraph is especially aimed at any dads who might be reading this book, but applies to anyone facing this decision: unless your career or business is a higher priority for you than your child's recovery, you *<u>should absolutely</u>* attend the training program with your spouse and be engaged the entire time. There truly shouldn't even be a question - other than perhaps "Do I use vacation time or FMLA time to attend?" Turn off the cell phone. Work will be waiting for you when the program is over. You could very well be one of the major keys to your child's recovery, but you will be significantly hindered if you rely on your spouse to try to translate what they have learned in a way that you'll be able to comprehend.

Of the four families that attended, only two of them had both spouses available for participation. In one instance, the husband who was working owned a restaurant and actually asked his wife to skip out on some training days to help work! Again, this exposed his true priorities. Another family had both parents there the first couple of days, but as the program went on they started tag-teaming the training sessions – only one would attend at a time, and they would trade off as though they were bearing a burden. It was no surprise to us that these families didn't experience the same level of success we did.

Buy in Early and Do More Than You Are Told

Despite reading some negative reviews on the parent training program, Melynda and I decided that we were going to buy in early and do whatever they told us to do, no matter how strange it sounded or how uncomfortable it made us. If this program was going to fail, we were determined to know that we had done everything we could to make it work and that we were not to blame for the failure. We soaked up every training session and made notes about how they could be improved for the future. If they asked us to experiment with a small walk around the neighborhood in a few days, we tried it that evening. We went to restaurants and endured screaming fits and disdainful glances (we were used to both, but had avoided the experience for some time) in order to practice what we were learning real-time. We bought duplicates of reinforcers that were working in the program, sometimes having to resort to eBay or flea markets to find a close match. We asked questions and dug in until we were satisfied with the answers. We held a firmer line in therapy sessions than we were required to hold (while sometimes breaking into tears once Timothy was out of sight). We honestly and legitimately gave the program 100% of our focus, attention, and effort, both in and out of the classroom, and this had a significant impact on Timothy's progress.

Unfortunately, not every family in the program did the same thing. One family had read a bunch of material on alternative therapies and biomedical interventions and seemed extremely skeptical about the program, consistently challenging the therapists in class as though they didn't know what they were talking about. This was also the family, coincidentally, that had both parents available but elected to send only one parent to most training sessions after a few days. They made some progress during the program, but it almost certainly could have been so much more.

Probably the saddest example, though, was the little girl in our class.

One of the things that TouchPoint did early on was ask us and the other families to feed their kids a light dinner and then bring them in the next morning after having had nothing but water for breakfast. In the early morning therapy sessions, the hungry children were offered a highly-preferred food (chips, in Timothy's case) as a reward for compliant behavior. This method quickly taught Timothy the value of compliance for rewards, and served as a framework for the ABA therapy system. Because we were very consistent and conscientious with this and did more than what we were asked, we only had to do this for a couple of days. Once Timothy "got it," we were able to quickly go off of food as a primary reinforcer, and move to a variety of toys that he enjoyed for the remainder of the program.

In contrast, during the last few days of the program, Melynda and I were having lunch and the mother of this little girl walked into the room with her daughter's lunch, most of it untouched. Her daughter had experienced little progress over the course of the program, and this session had gone no better. The therapist had instructed the mother to withhold a portion of the lunch until the following session. I still remember her exact words as she talked to us while putting away the lunch:

> "I really don't know what they think they're accomplishing with this. She just goes home and eats everything in sight."

Melynda and I were stunned into silence. This mother, who really needed to read the earlier section in this book about Tough Love, had been allowing her home environment to sabotage everything that was going on in the program. My heart weeps for the little girl, and I sincerely hope that someday they were able to "get it" and put their child through the temporary discomfort that is necessary to establish a beachhead for long-term life success. I fear, however, that she and thousands of other families may have institutionally violated the #1 rule of recovering from an ASD, which also happens to be Step 3 for ensuring the best possible TouchPoint Parent Training Program experience:

Don't Enable the Autism

Don't enable the Autism! TouchPoint taught us not to accept or excuse Timothy's inappropriate behavior, and explained how that could be the greatest force for destruction in his life. We were absolutely guilty of it, just like most parents are, and they gently showed us exactly what we were doing wrong and helped shape *our* behavior so that we could more effectively shape Timothy's. It was a hard reality to face, but we had to change our natural parenting style to meet the challenges of having an ASD-affected child.

TouchPoint gently challenged our ways of thinking. Timothy didn't have to be this way. Long-term, he didn't *want* to be this way. They helped us see that he would grow up and want a more normal life, but that if we didn't intentionally intervene, he might find himself without the skills required to have such a life. TouchPoint encouraged and enabled us to have a significant impact, to raise our expectations, but based on actual skills and knowledge being built in the classroom instead of on false hope. We learned to expect great things and work as though the outcome is inevitable, and that every child could improve.

5 Hidden Ways to Love Your Child With Autism

One thing about the folks at TouchPoint: they're very nice and respectful in the way they treat parents. They won't call you by your first name – it's all "Mr. and Mrs. Eden" and such. They keep you as a parent as the center and focal point of their work, which can be a refreshing change if you've been dealing with unhelpful school systems for some time.

The downside to this is that, sometimes, some parents need to be shaken up and told to stop doing what they're doing. Some parents need to have the dark realities painted for them that are inevitable if they continue on in their current patterns. But TouchPoint won't do that directly. I, on the other hand, as a fellow parent, absolutely will. They may well deny it, but here are the things TouchPoint taught me without having to say the words directly.

- Love your child enough to let them go hungry for a short time. (I would have doubled the time for Timothy early on if I would have thought we could have gotten half of the eventual results.)
- Love your child enough to let them be mad at you.
- Love your child enough to make them sad.
- Love your child enough to make life very unfair for them for a short number of years, so that it will be much easier for them over the span of their lifetime.

- Love your child enough to confront friends, family members, schools, government agencies, neighbors, strangers in stores and restaurants, and anyone else who tries to enable the Autism or just doesn't understand why you do what you do.

TouchPoint taught us how to stack the deck in our favor from a therapy perspective so that we and our other therapists could have the maximum impact. They also expended significant effort helping us learn how to choose our battles wisely, while making sure we knew the importance of never losing the critical ones at any cost. They taught us to think outside the box, to be willing to let a 20-minute session go more than an hour if that's what is required (assuming the extra time was not the *child's* goal). They showed us how to make dramatic improvements in Timothy's behavior by standing strong in the face of tears, screaming, crying, public embarrassment, and whatever else he decided to throw our way. We learned that embarrassment is temporary, but the gains in recovery made with a firm will on our part could last throughout Timothy's entire lifetime.

I walked away from the whole experience with the following message for the parents who will come after us in the program: **Whatever you do, don't be the thing that stood in the way of your child's recovery, particularly through enabling and rewarding the wrong behaviors.** Your child is *not* his or her autistic behaviors. You must believe there is a little kid inside them that wants to escape and be free. Help that child escape by standing up to the autistic behaviors – and win! You're bigger, faster, stronger, and smarter than they are – for now, anyway. You can absolutely do it – if you will.

TouchPoint also helped us recognize that each child's potential is different. You might not have the same rocket ship ride we had with Timothy, or his recovery may seem like a snail's pace compared to your experience. Your child may be more severely affected or may have other issues that complicate the ASD diagnosis, or may be further along than Timothy was at the beginning. The greatest thing that TouchPoint did was to encourage us to maximize what Timothy was capable of over his lifetime, and they gave us a deep understanding of the tools and therapies necessary to make that happen. Not only did we witness a quantum leap forward with Timothy's development in the program, but we came out armed for bear and ready to competently lead and aid our team of therapists down the continued road of his recovery.

I have no doubt that Timothy would have improved without the TouchPoint Parent Training Program. I also have no doubt that his recovery would have been greatly stunted by our own ignorance and the lack of structure we would have built into his life outside of the therapy room. I am eternally grateful to this program for what it enabled for Timothy's life, and my greatest hope is that every parent with an ASD-affected child can have the same experience we did so early in our own journey. It can mean the world to the whole family, but especially to your child.

Note: We believe so firmly in the value of this program that a portion of the proceeds of this book have been donated to TouchPoint's Angels for Autism fund. This fund provides scholarships for parents who otherwise could not afford to attend the Parent Training Program. If you would like more information or would like to make an additional donation to the fund or any of their other causes, you can get information at their website: http://TouchPointAutism.org.

Chapter 5: How to Build an Effective Therapy Program

How to Choose a Therapist

The key component of any strong therapy program is the people who do the work. If you are early in your journey, you are likely going to have to choose professionals in ABA, Occupational Therapy, Physical Therapy, Developmental Therapy, Speech/Language Therapy, and possibly Social/Emotional therapies as well. Here are some general guidelines to aid in your search.

- Your team should be heavily weighted with therapists that have ABA training and experience, even for those therapists doing non-ABA therapies. This perspective will make what they do in their own specialty infinitely more effective.
- You should have some non-ABA folks on your team as well. ABA is not a perfect panacea of therapy, and it is good to have trusted advisers who are skeptical of it and its approaches. While I generally disagreed with their assessments of ABA, I found that they tended to focus in areas that ABA folks didn't. That definitely enriched our therapy program for Timothy.
- Avoid zealots in any area. For example, many Social/Emotional therapists are so vested in their world view that they will proclaim ABA to cause more harm than it does good. There are also ABA therapists who feel the same way about Social/Emotional therapies. If you have alternatives, go with other professionals. You don't have room for closed minds when your child's future is at stake.

It is important to build a therapy team where everyone works together and can get along. It is equally important that you choose therapists who are willing to challenge and disagree with you as well. There have certainly been times in our journey when we thought Timothy had mastered a certain skill, only to find out that his "ability" was merely a learned, automatic response to a particular situation, and that if you changed the situation, the "skill" disappeared. This became especially apparent when we launched into Social/Emotional therapies. While these are never fun moments, it is critical that you arrive at a realistic assessment of your child's true situation. As painful as this can be, just because your child can be polite, respond to questions, and greet people appropriately with eye contact does *not* mean that he or she is actually functionally communicating with another person. You need to have therapists who are willing to tell you that, and on the other side, therapists who built that skill who can hear that feedback without taking it personally.

What to Do if You Choose the Wrong Therapist

Our first speech/language therapist is a good example of a poor decision based on convenience and logistics. Her style was very laid back, and Timothy manipulated her easily. We felt like his other therapists were better at getting him to communicate than she was. While I'm sure her style might be a good fit for some kids, it was quickly obvious to both Melynda and me that this was not an optimal situation for Timothy.

Firing a therapist is hard to do. After all, you are not an expert in their field, and they are, and you are making judgments based on their effectiveness. The most important thing to remember is to trust your instincts and act quickly. The therapist may be very knowledgeable, but that does not make him or her a good fit for your child. No one is more of an expert on your child than you are, and if you recognize that a particular style is counter-productive, it's better to act quickly and replace them with a more effective person.

If the therapist works for an agency or are representatives of a government program, you can usually call that agency or your coordinator and let them know that you don't feel the therapist is a good fit for your family. You usually won't need to give any more explanation than that, and no direct contact with the therapist is required. If you are dealing directly with the therapist, the situation is a lot harder, since you'll need to tell the person directly that you won't be using their services any more. Most professionals will simply take the "not a good fit" answer, end the call politely, and move on. If you get someone who wants more justification, just remember that they asked for it, but try to keep the feedback professional. Beware of any guilty feelings on your part that the therapist may use to ask for "one more chance." This situation almost never works out, and only prolongs the time period when your child is being served with less than optimal therapy. Once you've made the decision to move on, don't go back. Your original instincts are almost always right.

9 Personalities You Should Seek Out for Your Team

While you may have a sense for a completely bad fit and should act quickly, you also don't want to build a team where everyone has the same personality and skill sets. There is power in diversity! Learn to appreciate different personalities. Your child needs them all for different reasons. Folks that are ineffective at one stage in the process may be exactly what is needed in another. Folks that are effective early on may become less so as time goes on. You should intentionally seek out a wide range of backgrounds and personalities to meet your child's various needs. The list below is a general overview of the types we employed on our own team:

1. **The Drill Sergeant:** Early on, it is critical to establish control. We needed a "heartless" dictator who did not emotionally respond to crying, tantrums, gagging (even vomiting) or other manipulative tactics. This person on our team became famous for making Timothy walk the line for everything from eating carrots and going

on walks in the neighborhood to curbing self-stimulatory behaviors.

Timothy had a severe obsessive behavior around doors, and most therapists simply pried them open with safety gates that Timothy could not remove so that they could work with him. Not the Drill Sergeant! He would intentionally leave doors partially open and accessible, and then work the entire session as much on not touching the door as any other program. This approach helped significantly reduce this bad habit and allowed us to slowly remove restrictions in Timothy's environment.

The Drill Sergeant was a critical resource in our early months of therapy to get the ground rules established quickly with our son. Once ground rules were established, however, this rigid approach started to lose its effectiveness. When we were beginning to move away from the militaristic, solid lines of ABA and into the fuzzier, more touchy-feely world of Social/Emotional therapies, the Drill Sergeant had a tougher time than most. That said, we likely would have taken a lot longer to get to that point if it hadn't been for his influence.

2. **The Little Engine That Could:** This person was extremely high energy, optimistic, and tough. She met Timothy's obstinate attitudes and game-playing with pure love and infinite energy. Once she started down a path with Timothy with a specific goal in mind, the poor boy never stood a chance. She broke down barriers, wouldn't take any of his crap, and wouldn't accept anything less than Timothy's best. Very early on she believed his best was nothing short of excellence, and she pushed and pushed hard to get him to reach that potential.

This was her natural mode of operation, which spilled over into her dealings with us as well. She was extremely passionate about her areas of expertise, none of which were related to ABA. There were times when she and I disagreed on how to approach certain areas. Rather than simply letting things go, she pushed us hard on our assumptions and made us prove her wrong if we thought she was. There were times when, after examining the evidence, I had to admit that she was right. There were also times when the opposite was true, and I must admit, she was much more gracious in admitting she was wrong than I was.

Even though she did not have an ABA background, she exerted tremendous influence over Timothy's ABA programming. The tools and techniques she used were extremely powerful, and we made sure they were utilized as much as possible across his various therapy types. She was a great person to have at an initial IEP – again, you knew from the start that she wasn't going to tolerate games. Like the Drill Sergeant, she was critical in Timothy's early phases of recovery, but she possessed the ability to shift gears as his needs changed and remained a critical part of the team for years.

3. **The Administrator:** This team member knew the rules of IEPs and IFSPs better than the teachers and administrators running the meetings, and we had her in as many of them as possible in the early days. She was aware of every program availability and every option that we could pursue and was a critical part of preparing for these meetings. We made sure she was plugged into every part of Timothy's therapy process, whether it was home, school, or otherwise. Outside of Melynda and me, she was the hub around which all other therapies flowed, even when she did not directly control the therapists.

One of the things we appreciated most about her was that she was very direct. If we asked a question, we got a straight, unambiguous answer. Twenty-minute conversations with her got us farther in many cases than weeks of research on our own. She was the one we relied on to discuss strategies for Timothy's therapy plans, IEPs and IFSPs, and even decisions like where to move when our lease ran out. She wasn't afraid to tell us the unvarnished truth, and she had many years of experience that we could rely on. Having her on the team saved us a *lot* of time.

She also approached Timothy's therapies with the same precision and expertise. She could easily switch roles from parent consultant to therapist to child advocate and back. She had a great sense for Timothy's capabilities, when to push, and when to back off and return to fight another day. If we had to do it all over again on a desert island with only one therapist available, she would be the one we would choose.

4. **The Big Sister:** This person formed a special bond with Timothy
    via play skills in a way that was mysterious and almost magical.
    She was comfortable with lots of close physical contact, which I
    believe aided in the emotional bonding process. She also generally
    pushed him a little harder than the average therapist was willing to
    do. She was no Drill Sergeant, but she commanded respect
    nonetheless.

    One of the best things about her was her willingness to mix up
    Timothy's routines and experiment without being asked. Once
    going on walks had been established, she was the one who would
    stop to smell flowers, look at ants on the sidewalk, or watch the
    birds in the trees. She taught Timothy to play simple songs on a
    small keyboard. She read books to him and would stop and ask
    him novel questions about things that would interest him. In fact,
    that was one of her biggest strengths: she found ways to reach him
    by seeing what he was already interested in and pushing that
    interest to the next level.

    She came to us about halfway through our initial major therapy
    push. This was OK, as I'm not sure she would have been nearly as
    effective with Timothy early on in our therapy journey, but she
    was certainly someone in the right place at the right time for him.

5. **The Goofy Big Brother:** This was the first person outside of our
    family to form a legitimate emotional bond with Timothy. He was
    around early in Timothy's therapy journey, and frankly, he wasn't
    that effective in the early days. He had a lax style, some silly
    behaviors, and was definitely not the toughest therapist on the
    team. He was good enough that we didn't let him go (frankly, we
    needed as many hours as we could get), but our initial impressions
    of him didn't reflect a top-tier therapist.

    We were dead wrong. As Timothy progressed and started showing
    sparks of personality, it was the Goofy Big Brother that drew it out
    of him like no one else could. They developed little routines,
    games, and inside jokes that stretched Timothy's social skills in
    ways we would never have imagined at the time. Timothy would
    beg for this guy to come around so that he could repeat their silly

games, and to everyone's amazement, Timothy eventually started making them up on his own! (Today, Timothy has pretty good skills as an improv singer...) There was something special about watching them talk – the Goofy Big Brother honestly and openly sharing about his day, and Timothy coming up with new, sneaky ways to make him laugh. It was like nothing I had ever seen.

As we transitioned away from strict behavioral approaches and more towards Social/Emotional therapies, the Goofy Big Brother and the Big Sister were our two all-stars. The Big Sister was better at structuring environments, but no one could engage Timothy like the Goofy Big Brother. The Social/Emotional approaches came very naturally for him too, and seemed like a better fit than the ABA therapies had been.

6. **The Dreamer:** This person was trained in both ABA and Social/Emotional therapies. While she understood the philosophical differences, she believed that the different therapies were compatible, just good at different things. Not a loud person, but not afraid of strong personalities. She was tough on us, not letting us believe that Timothy was farther along than he really was, but this enabled us to face reality and take appropriate measures, with fantastic results.

She was comfortable dealing with abstractions and letting us struggle through issues that were either mushy or uncomfortable. She was willing to experiment and try new things. She, more than anyone, pushed us outside of our comfort zone as Timothy's needs evolved. As we were faced with the prospect of unlearning ways of communicating with him that we had spent months building to a point of success, she would remind us of what the real world would be like for Timothy and kept us on task. She never stopped looking towards the next horizon.

She was an incredibly effective Social/Emotional therapist, and we made great strides under her leadership. She also helped give us a perspective about Timothy's development compared to typical peers, and helped us know what *not* to focus on to help aid in the transitions that school would bring. She added a whole different dimension to IEPs, and we made sure she was there as much as we could.

As Timothy's rocket towards normalcy continued, she was the one that encouraged us to start considering the possibility that we wouldn't need her or the other therapists any more. When the time was right, like a mother bird pushing a baby bird out of a nest, she pushed us to move towards accepting normalcy, and away from reliance on in-home therapists. If anyone had an equivalent effect on us as the TouchPoint Parent Training Program, it was the Dreamer.

7. **The Nannies:** We were fortunate enough to have several of these on the team: consistent, dependable, predictable, very "in-the-box," but willing to try new things if requested and shown how. Once a successful pattern had been established with other therapists, they were a crucial part of exposing Timothy to predictable and consistent environments as his skills advanced.

These individuals exhibited special skills in getting Timothy integrated into community environments once he was ready. Trips to parks, swimming pools, grocery stores, and restaurants were performed over and over again and allowed us to slowly move towards normal life patterns. They were very consistent at carrying over programs from Timothy's Speech/Language and Occupational therapists. The core of Timothy's therapy was built on these individuals.

They were generally the best folks at keeping good records, making sure that everyone else was documenting sessions correctly and mastering out programs when appropriate. They helped keep us on track and were a great early-warning system if other therapists weren't doing what they needed to do for legal reasons. In many ways, they were Melynda's right-hand people. They were all very helpful, and we could not have accomplished what we did without them.

8. **The Enforcer (a.k.a. Bad Cop):** Every good hockey team has an enforcer to defend the other players from attacks. Every good "Good Cop" is accompanied by an equally effective "Bad Cop." This was the role I got to play. When it came to IEPs and IFSPs, I was the guy who made the tough statements in meetings so that the therapists, who would have to work with these people long after we were gone, wouldn't have to. I was willing to "enter the danger zone" in a meeting and openly challenge assumptions that were being thrown out. I was also willing to call someone on the carpet if they overstepped boundaries. If something uncomfortable needed to be said, I took it upon myself to say it.

    In one situation we had arranged for our Administrator therapist to observe Timothy in his classroom. The main teacher happened to call in sick that day and had forgotten to tell anyone that our therapist was coming. When she got there, she was told to leave since no one knew she was allowed to be there and they didn't know we had given our blessing. The mistake was they did this without calling us to confirm. Keep in mind, we were paying for this person's time, and everyone there knew she was one of Timothy's key therapists. I learned about the situation about 30 minutes later when our therapist called to let us know what had happened. While it was incredibly uncomfortable, I picked up the phone, called the school, asked to speak to the person responsible, and let them know that the next time they sent one of my therapists away without checking with me first, they were going to have a lot more to deal with than an angry phone call. They got the message, apologized profusely, and the next time our therapist went in, she reported that she had never been treated with more respect.

    I was the one responsible for defending my team: my family, my therapists, and our aggressive hopes for Timothy's recovery. Needless to say, I was not always popular with teachers and administrators (or the condo board) who were unaccustomed to being challenged in a logical, fact-based way. Every good team needs someone who can play this role when it is required.

9. **The Central Hub:** This was the role my wife played. She was the one who kept normalized, ongoing relationships and dialogue with teachers and therapists. They could sympathize with her having to deal with such an "overbearing" husband (if only they knew!) She

is a naturally details-oriented person who kept everything we were trying to do for Timothy all together. She tracked everyone's hours, made detailed records of therapist availability and school schedules, and was generally the go-to person if someone needed to know what was going on with anyone at any point in time, or what was coming up soon.

Melynda made sure that therapeutic goals were consistent across the various types of therapies. She was usually the first person a therapist talked to when they arrived in our home, and she made a point to update them on the latest behavior challenge or tool or technique we were trying to implement. She was also the last person they would talk to, and she would use that time to get updates on progress and tidbits to pass along to the next person on the schedule. She read every journal entry that our therapists wrote and made sure to put corrective notes if folks got off track. As a result, that almost never happened, and when it did, the time period was extremely short. She was simply on it, all the time.

Melynda was also the person who made sure our daughter Emily was part of the team and felt fully included. She made sure to spend time specifically with her, and helped me adjust my schedule so that I could do the same. In the hurricane that was Timothy's therapy program, Melynda was the eye of the storm, the calm center around which everything and everyone else flowed – including me. Without her, the rest of our efforts would have largely been best defined as random acts of remediation. Because of her, we had a consistent, powerful team in which everyone was pulling in the same direction all the time. Her impact is incalculable.

Like all great teams, it's impossible to imagine how anything we did could have been a success without every single one of the individuals above and their contributions to Timothy's ongoing emergence from Autism. I strongly encourage you to make sure you've got at least one person on your team that represents each of these stereotypes. You'll have a stronger program for it.

2 Critical Steps to Engage Older Siblings

In the best of circumstances sibling relationships can be stressful when the kids are young. Throw a younger special-needs sibling into the mix, with social problems and the need for lots of special attention, and you've got a potential recipe for jealousy, resentment, and a lot of added stress.

We understood this reality from the beginning. Emily was 7 ½ years old when we got Timothy's diagnosis. She already had a unique relationship with him that we wanted to leverage, if possible. We wanted her to feel like an important part of the team that was helping to bring her little brother out of his enclosed, silent world. Here are the strategies we employed.

Don't Pretend That Nothing Has Changed

Kids are not dumb. They will notice the amount of time and energy you spend on the other child, and the difference that makes in your availability for them. Nearly the worst thing you can do is try to hide it. The absolute worst thing you can do is try to apologize for it. Trying to minimize what is happening will merely give your older child or children a sense that they are being cheated in some way, which can magnify any resentment they might feel. Even worse, some kids in this situation may try to play off of your guilty feelings for their personal gain. They're kids, after all. It's what they do best. Unfortunately, this not only increases your stress levels, it doesn't really do them any good in the long run.

While there are some costs involved, having a special-needs younger sibling should also be viewed as an *opportunity* for your other children. In our culture of "me first," these kids will have a first-hand, real-world opportunity to learn how to lead through service. Nothing impacted Emily's character development more positively than having a younger brother with Autism. She learned to adapt to his needs, to see the world through his eyes, and this made her a better person. She was a better friend

71

to other kids at school, a more helpful daughter, and socially matured in ways that may not have happened had it not been for Timothy.

Having a special-needs brother also allowed her access to special events and activities geared towards older siblings like her. She loved going to "sib shops" put on by our various support organizations. She instantly had things in common with new people she met who also had younger siblings on the spectrum. She was able to present herself as an expert, relative to her peers, on the subject of Autism, which gave her opportunities to develop additional leadership and public speaking skills.

In summary, the changes weren't all bad, and from a personal growth standpoint in particular, they were extremely valuable. Emily is a better person today because of Timothy's influence in her life. I would say the same is true for me, and for many of the same reasons.

Make Them an Integral Part of the Team – Or Else!

Emily had always wanted a little brother or sister. While a significant factor for this desire was to have a playmate, it was also obvious to us that she wanted someone to "take care of." Emily liked being in control of situations, and was naturally skilled in that area. By the time she was 3 years old, we had to tell her to stop manipulating other relatives and adults who watched her, and warn the adults about her tactics.

When we realized what we were up against with Timothy, we decided to take Emily's natural tendencies and use them to our advantage. From the beginning, we taught her everything we knew about therapy. We taught her how to talk to Timothy, how to praise and reprimand, and how to actively ignore when he misbehaved. We gave her as much authority over him as she could appropriately handle. She helped us enforce behaviors and perform activities in the car when we couldn't reach him. She joined us and other therapists for therapy times (as long as she wasn't a distraction). We leveraged their special bond and coached her in how to intentionally build play skills in him. She was at one time a playful big sister, a therapist, and a third parent for Timothy all rolled up into one.

Emily reinforced what Timothy was learning – albeit imperfectly at times given her age – more consistently than any other person besides my wife. They shared a bedroom, so through the slats of his crib she was the last person he saw before going to sleep and the first person he saw when he woke up. Having her as a positive influence on Timothy was a critical part of his success story. Making her such a crucial part of the team and regularly recognizing her accomplishments in this mitigated most of the resentment that might have built up. Timothy's journey wasn't something she had to watch from the outside. She was a key part of the process! Frankly, I'm not sure how we could have done it without her, and that realization on your part is probably the most powerful weapon you have when trying to deal with sibling relationships.

Train them. Give them tools. Give them as much responsibility and authority as they can handle. Let them fail, then coach them towards better results in the future. If you try to protect or insulate them from the process, you only cast them as outsiders, which will serve to make the resentment more profound. Lavish praise on them and never let them forget how important they are to their younger sibling's progress. In the end, everyone ends up winning, sometimes in ways you won't see coming.

3 Ways to Stretch Therapy Supply Dollars

An effective team needs the right tools to be successful, and it's your job as a parent to make sure they have what they need. We realized early on that we were going to require lots and lots of various kinds of supplies, reinforcer toys, and therapeutic equipment to push forward with our overall strategy. While we got a few things from other parents and grandparents, most of Timothy's supplies were purchased by us. Since we definitely did not have limitless resources, we had to figure out ways to make those dollars stretch. Here are the three biggest things that helped us do just that.

Frequent Lots of Dollar Stores

We quickly found that we needed more toys for various settings, and
especially once our in-home ABA program was in full swing we needed
lots of novel reinforcer toys. Although stores like Target and Wal-Mart
had many great toys, they were typically each $15-30 or more. We needed
to buy ten or more new items at one time, and we were on a budget. Dollar
stores filled with cheaply-made toys were frequent targets on our search for
reinforcers and supplies. They offered a seemingly limitless supply of
cheap containers, small toys, and games, and art supplies. Different dollar
stores carry vastly different inventories. This was also sometimes true of
different locations within the same chain. The items purchased tended to be
lower quality, but we didn't care if a toy or therapy item wouldn't last more
than a couple of months. Timothy was generally tired of them before they
wore out anyway.

Buy Second Hand

Resale shops were invaluable to us for about a three-year time period. The
toys for Timothy did not have to be the latest and greatest - they just had to
be varied and different, with lots of buttons, colors, lights, and obnoxious
music. What dollar stores didn't offer, we could usually find at a resale
shop for $3-5 per toy. When Timothy grew tired of certain toys, we
cleaned them up and returned them to a resale shop. The resale shop
would usually buy them from us, and we would have a bit of a credit to use
on our next batch of toys.

Other treasure troves included thrift stores like Goodwill, flea markets,
garage sales, and web sites like Craigslist. Ebay was also useful, but we
found it has many supply vendors who are selling their supplies at full
price. Google searches were particularly useful if we were looking for a
discontinued toy that seemed to catch and hold Timothy's attention. We

would try searching by product name, product number, serial number, character names, and just about anything else we could think of on the off chance that someone would have one for sale.

Get Creative

At one point we needed a baseball on a string (pendulum ball system) to work on coordination and visual integration. These systems online sell for $50, up to hundreds of dollars for complete kits. Instead, we went to a retail store and bought two wall hooks, a ceiling hook, a wiffle ball and bat, and some kite string and built it ourselves for just over $10.

We scoured garage sales and the previously mentioned dollar stores for different sizes of exercise and sensory balls. We used a simple wooden board standing on different objects to work on balance. We bought cheap toy disco balls and rotating lights for $10 on clearance. We searched the Internet for deals on collapsible nylon tunnels and inflatable ball pits. Generally we found that, if we ever felt we needed some expensive sensory therapy item, we could usually come up with a reasonable alternative for a fraction of the cost of the therapy equivalent.

The key was to figure out what the benefit of the item was going to be and asking what alternatives we had for achieving close to the same thing. Were our alternatives always as effective? Probably not, but by my estimation we were normally within 80-85% as effective as the high-priced alternative. When it came to supplies, 80-85% was close enough, and the money we saved was much better spent on actual time with therapists rather than the fancy toys.

Goals in Concrete, Plans in Sand

This book contains a lot of hard-knock practical advice. Some of it may not apply to your situation – for example, being a single parent or having younger siblings for your child with autism undoubtedly limits your options in ways I can only imagine. You may not get the diagnosis until the child is older, perhaps already in school. These scenarios definitely complicate the strategy development process! That said, the principles should not change. Learn how to read your environment and fully understand your situation. Learn how to evaluate therapies. Understand the possible range of motives for your child's helpers. Understand that this is a war, one that can be largely won if fought correctly, and pour yourself into this battle for at least a couple of years. Most importantly though, in the midst of this struggle, don't allow it to swallow you completely. Keep your priorities in line. Stay close to your spouse and your other kids. Resist the urge to withdraw in your suffering. Look at this as just another part of your journey – one that will always be with you, but not one that has to define you in a negative sense. Set the stage for your own miracle, and then trust in God and in your child to take care of the rest. You have an entire community rooting for you, and so am I. Good luck, and God bless.

ABOUT THE AUTHOR

Jason Eden is a husband and father, a musician, and a teacher. He has more than a decade of experience in corporate education and holds an M.B.A. from the Olin Business School in Saint Louis, MO, as well as a Bachelor's Degree in Psychology from Southwest Baptist University in Bolivar, MO. He serves on a Human Rights Council for Behavior Intervention Services in Saint Louis and has frequently served as a guest speaker for autism-related group events.

Learn more at http://www.MidstOfAMiracle.com.

Made in the USA
Charleston, SC
26 October 2011